Carving Cypress Knee Wood Spirits

Al Streetman

AF271651

Schiffer Publishing Ltd

4880 Lower Valley Road, Atglen, PA 19310 USA

Copyright © 2002 by Al Streetman
Library of Congress Control Number: 2001095973

All rights reserved. No part of this work may be reproduced or used in any form or by any means—graphic, electronic, or mechanical, including photocopying or information storage and retrieval systems—without written permission from the copyright holder.

"Schiffer," "Schiffer Publishing Ltd. & Design," and the "Design of pen and ink well" are registered trademarks of Schiffer Publishing Ltd.

Designed by "Sue"
Type set in Zapf Humanist Bd BT/Lydian BT

ISBN: 0-7643-1518-8
Printed in China
1 2 3 4

Published by Schiffer Publishing Ltd.
4880 Lower Valley Road
Atglen, PA 19310
Phone: (610) 593-1777; Fax: (610) 593-2002
E-mail: Schifferbk@aol.com
Please visit our web site catalog at www.schifferbooks.com
We are always looking for people to write books on new and related subjects. If you have an idea for a book please contact us at the above address.

This book may be purchased from the publisher.
Include $3.95 for shipping.
Please try your bookstore first.
You may write for a free catalog.

In Europe, Schiffer books are distributed by
Bushwood Books
6 Marksbury Ave.
Kew Gardens
Surrey TW9 4JF England
Phone: 44 (0)20-8392-8585
Fax: 44 (0)20-8392-9876
E-mail: Bushwd@aol.com
Free postage in the UK. Europe: air mail at cost

Contents

Acknowledgments

The following people helped make this book possible. I thank you all.

Tim and Debbie Effrem, Woodcarvers Supply, Inc. (1-800-284-6229): For graciously providing the excellent quality tools I am using on my current projects. They carry an outstanding assortment of fine carving tools, supplies, and books.

Michael Cuomo: (csknees@cypressknees.itgo.com). Thank you for so generously providing the cypress knees used in this book. Michael Cuomo has a great selection of cypress knees at bargain prices.

DecoArt: As always, the paint samples were excellent, and satisfactory in all respects.

Royal Brush Mfg., Inc. DecoArt carries excellent quality paintbrushes at affordable prices.

Introduction

For those of you who are used to sawing out a blank from a pattern and taking it to the finished stage, this book will offer something different, and possibly new to you. This time, we are going to turn a raw cypress knee into a full-size Santa, and also we will carve an icicle Santa ornament. Cypress knees are great for items such as Santas, because the natural wrinkles in the wood look just like folds and wrinkles in clothing . . . you don't have to do a lot of creative gouge work to achieve the look. In order to accomplish carvings of this type, you have to let the cypress knee "talk" to you. There is no real pattern to follow, except the pattern that suggests itself to you as you look at the cypress knee from all sides and angles. Once you order and receive your knees, take them out and look them over. Each one is unique, both in size and shape. Sometimes, you will see the Santa or other character immediately in the wrinkles and folds of the knee, and other times it won't be so obvious. Remember, these wood spirits are mischievous, and occasionally they will hide for a while before revealing themselves. For the ornery knees, just set them aside for a day or two. Eventually, as you look at them from time to time, you will finally see the hidden character reveal itself, and you can get to work freeing it from the knee.

I obtain my raw cypress knees from Michael Cuomo (please see the acknowledgments at the front of this book for further information). When you order them, ask for the ones that have already been boiled and peeled. They only cost a tiny bit more than the ones that you would have to peel yourself, but the savings in time on your part is invaluable. This allows you to get to work carving them as soon as you get them. They are relatively inexpensive, and they carve like a dream.

We will go through two projects in full detail, from carving to painting to finishing.

Some of you may observe that these carving projects are not as complex or detailed as you might wish to carve them. *There is a method to my madness.* In this book, as in all of my previous books, I have tried to design projects that would yield nice results, yet not be so complex or involved that the *beginning wood carver* would not be able to complete them. I want to reach as many wood carvers as possible and share the joy of carving with them all. As beginners gain more experience, they can add additional details as desired.

Except for the actual carving projects, I have not included specific carving instructions. I have found that each carver has his or her own style, and each has their preference for which tool to use in a particular area, or to achieve a particular effect.

Rather than giving a vague instruction such as "use a small gouge," I have listed the particular size tool I used in each step of the carving project. This is more for the benefit of the beginning carver, rather than the more experienced ones. If you don't have gouges or tools in these particular sizes, use something similar.

General Notes

1. *I recommend that you read the entire book before starting the project.* This will help you see where we are going, and will help alert you to carving techniques that may be unfamiliar. In the section where we paint the project, you may see an area or detail that might not have been clear to you in the carving section. Reading the entire book through before beginning the project will help you identify any such areas, and may help eliminate frustration at a later time. Remember, if we carve it, we will paint it, so you will see everything at least twice.

2. Before starting your carving, ensure that you have your tools as sharp as possible. If you haven't stropped your knives and gouges in a while, do it now. I know, ...it's a pain in the rear, and it takes away precious time that you could be using to carve something, but it makes the actual carving time so much more pleasant. I don't like to do it either, but I definitely hate working with dull tools! If you can try to get in the habit of sharpening and honing your tools at least once a week, you will find that you actually have more hours of real carving time in the long run.

Project Carving Tools

For those of you who may want to duplicate the cuts I made using the same tools I used, I have listed the tools used in the carving project. If you are already an experienced carver, then most likely you have some favorite tools that you prefer to use in order to achieve the desired results and effects. New carvers are sometimes overwhelmed by the variety of carving tools and accessories available in different stores and catalogs. Before you go out and take a second mortgage on the ranch just to finance all the tools you 'think' you will need to get the job accomplished, try this approach: purchase a fixed-blade bench knife (fairly long wooden handle with about a 1-1/2" long blade, a couple of "V" gouges (perhaps 1/8" and 1/4"), and a couple of "U" gouges. Learn how to sharpen them, because they do not normally come ready to use, no matter what the catalogs may say. Dull knives and gouges are one of the leading causes of frustration for new carvers, because they haven't realized yet that the dullness of their tools is causing the problem. This is the point that some would-be great carvers give up and move on to needle-point or something else less intimidating. There are many good books on the market that will tell you in words, and show you with photos, how to get the proper edge on the various types of knives and gouges.

Once you have learned how to put a good edge on your tools, maintaining that edge will then only require a mild stropping. You will, of course, have to put the tool on a sharpening stone occasionally, but unless you have dropped the tool or otherwise damaged the edge, most of the time a light stropping will be all that is required.

After working diligently to make sure your tools are sharp, look at the effects the "V" gouge and the "U" gouge can create. You may even want to make some practice cuts on some scrap wood, in order to observe the various effects that can be achieved with each type of tool. Whichever tool type best suits your likes and is the most visually appealing to you, then that is the type to obtain more of to round out your arsenal.

I mainly use a "V" gouge to outline areas I want to remove wood from, and to create things such as wrinkles and soles on shoes; but, personally I find that I use the "U" type gouges much more frequently. The results produced with "U" gouges on areas such as hair and beards suit me more than the results achieved with "V" gouges. You may feel that the "V" does a better job for you, and it is your right to feel that way. There is no "correct" tool to use, except the one that gives the effect that makes you the happiest. It's all a part of the personal "style" that you have, or that you will develop. I have been using tools from Wood Carver's Supply in Englewood, Florida, recently. These tools are of excellent quality and priced very reasonably. If you aren't sure which tool would be best for you, give them a call. They will work with you on the phone to ensure that you get just the right item(s).

#39 3 mm 60 degree true "V" gouge
#39 4.5 mm 60 degree true "V" gouge
#9 4.5 mm deep "U" gouge
#9 6 mm deep "U" gouge
#1 10 mm straight gouge.
General Whittling knife, 1-1/8" blade

General Painting Suggestions and Paintbrush Recommendations

I have included some suggestions for colors and paint brushes. If you have a preference for a different color scheme, by all means use it. After all, it's your carving, and you are free to paint it any way you desire.

I have also listed the colors produced by DecoArt and their identification numbers, which I have found to be suitable for painting these carvings. I have used these colors, and the results are excellent. I hope this will help minimize your confusion when trying to sort through the maze of paint brands and colors at your hobby or craft store.

The best paintbrushes I have found, for the money, are made by the Royal Brush Mfg. Company. They come in a wide assortment of sizes and shapes, are durable, and most importantly, are affordable. In general, here are the ones I use and recommend for painting your carvings.

Royal Golden Taklon series 250 Round, size 0 and 00: Details such as eyes and other small areas.

Royal Golden Taklon series 170 Cat's Tongue, size 2 and 4: Large areas.

Royal Golden Taklon series 150 Short Shader, size 2 and 4: Blending colors (for example, when blending a "blush" color into the flesh color on faces, hands, etc.).

Suggested Colors for the Carving Projects

Titanium White DA1; Lamp Black DA67; Country Blue DA41; Santa Red DA170
Reindeer Moss Green DA187; French Vanilla DA184; Blush Flesh DA110
Flesh Tone DA78; Burnt Sienna DA63; Raw Sienna DA93
Shimmering Silver DA70; DuraClear Satin Varnish DS21; Walnut Gel Stain DS29

Additional Colors You May Want To Try

Avocado DA52; Camel DA191; Buttermilk DA3; Napthol Red DA104
Navy Blue DA35; Desert Sand DA77; Taffy Cream DA5; Glorious Gold DA71
Emperor's Gold DA148

If you cannot find these colors locally, you can contact DecoArt at: (http://www.decoart.com). They will be glad to tell you where a dealer is located close to you, and in many cases will provide you with samples of some of the colors for you to try.

Remember: These are only a few of the many colors you can use for your carvings. Should you have other color preferences, use them. Don't be afraid to get wild and experiment with all sorts of color combinations. For those of you (like me), who have difficulty trying to decide which colors work well together, most hobby and art supply stores sell inexpensive color wheels which will show you colors that work together, and colors that oppose each other.

I have listed a few combinations here, for illustrative purposes:

Main Color	Contrast Color
Red	Green
Orange	Blue
Yellow	Violet

A good color wheel will not only show you main and contrast colors, it will also show colors that blend.

"Antiquing" the Project

Once the paint is dry, you may want to "age" your carving with an antiquing product in order to help tone down the colors a bit. I have had excellent results using antiquing gels made by DecoArt. These are available at hobby and craft stores. They come in various colors, so you can create different effects.

Brush a coat of antiquing gel on the wood, then wipe it off using a damp rag or sponge. It is your option how much you wipe off. After the antiquing is dry, I like to finish my carvings with a coat of brush-on acrylic varnish. DecoArt also makes an excellent varnish. I prefer the one that leaves a Satin finish. This particular finish is not too flat nor too glossy, but leaves a "soft" look to the completed carving. *(I usually put a coat of varnish on the face, hands, and other flesh areas BEFORE I antique the carving)*. This will prevent these areas from absorbing too much antiquing color.

Carving the Projects

Carving the Full-Size Santa

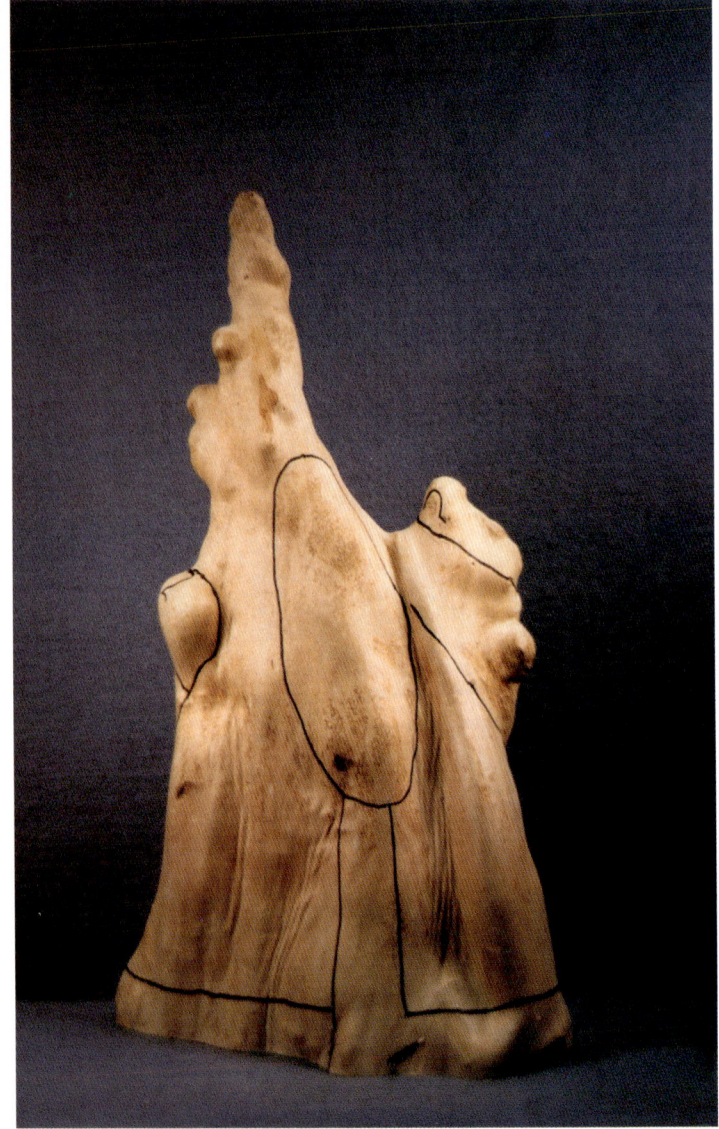

Here is the knee that I selected to carve. It may not be obvious to you in this photo where I see the Santa, but look at the next photo and see if you were thinking along the same lines as me. If you saw something different, don't worry. That's what makes the cypress knees so much fun. Everyone will see different characters in them, so your carvings will always be original!

In this photo, I have used a fine-line marker pen to sketch in the Santa shape that jumped out at me. (NOTE: At this point, before you start carving, examine the bottom of the knee. These are cut from the swamp with a chainsaw, and often the bottom is not quite square or flat. If yours are like that, place them on a belt sander and briefly sand the bottom until they are flat. If you do this before you start carving, you won't risk damaging the finished carving later.)

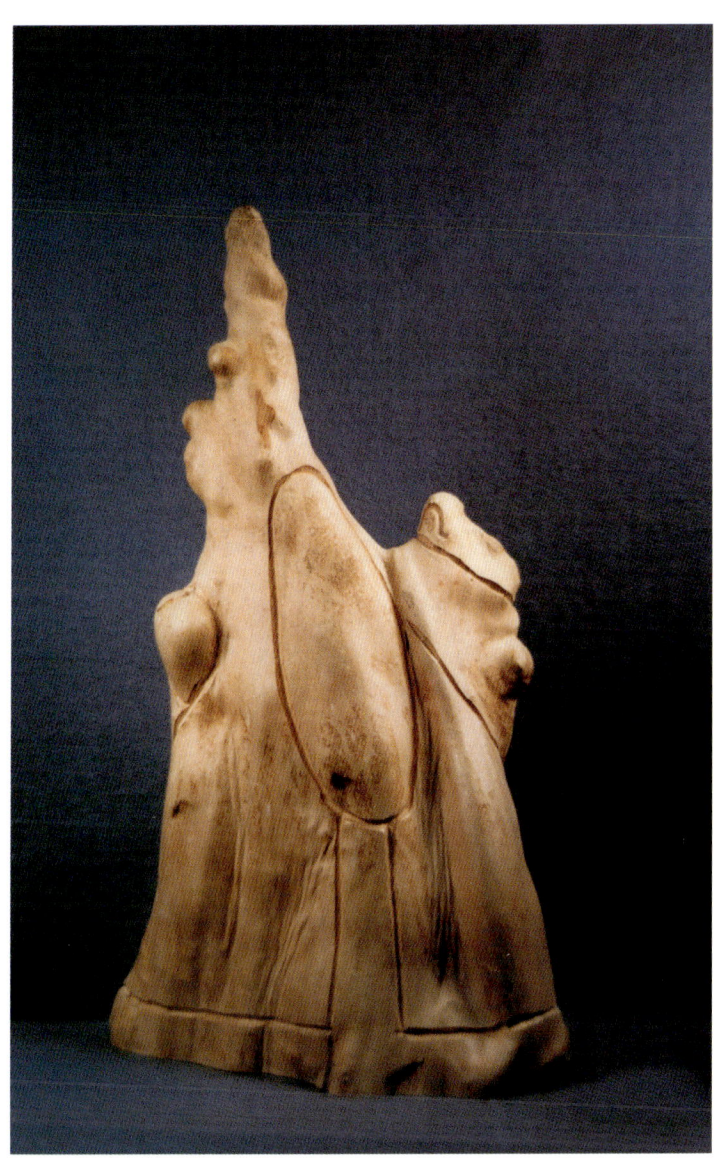

Go over all the lines with a 4.5 mm 60 degree "V" gouge to further define the key areas on the Santa. We'll clean them up as we go along, but for now, we'll work on the face area.

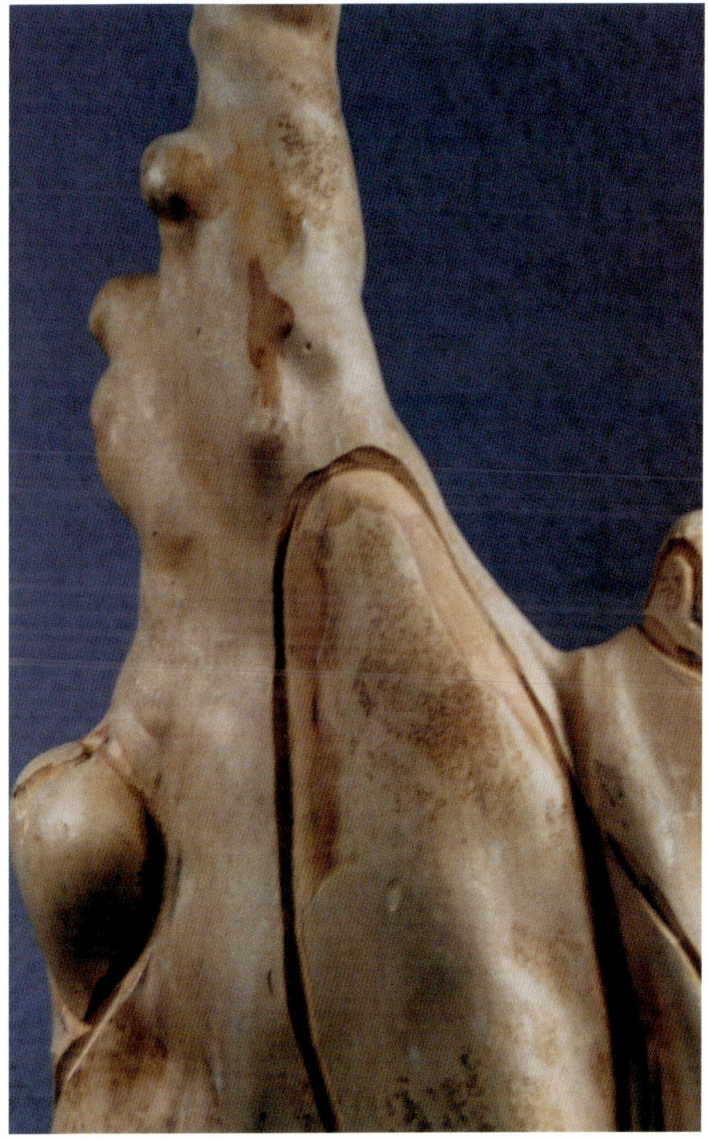

Use your knife to shave away some wood so the face and upper beard area stands out from the hood and body.

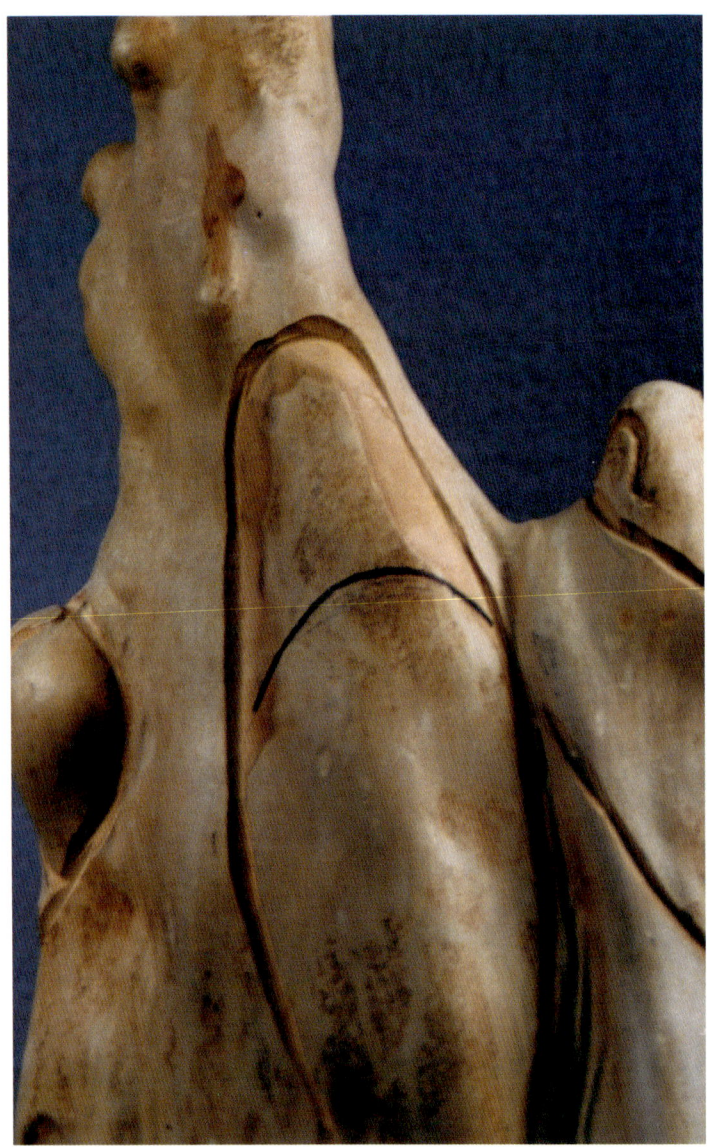

Now let's get a face on this ol' rascal. We are going to do this using one of Uncle Al's E-Z Santa face techniques. Identify where you want the top of the cheeks to be. (This will change from carving to carving, at your option and as dictated by the amount of wood area you have for the face). Sketch in a curved line as seen here to establish the initial definition for the top of the cheeks, so we can get an idea where to locate the eyes.

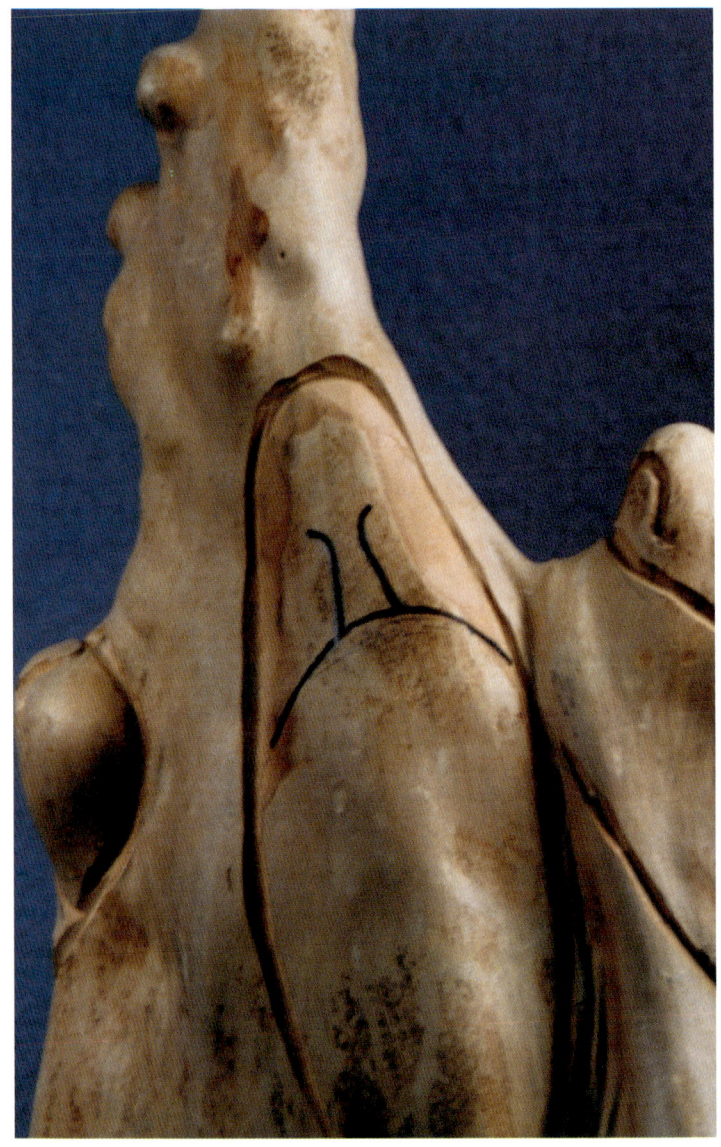

Next, sketch in two lines up the middle of the face and curving out, as seen here. These define the sides of the nose, and the top of the eye area. This is yet another area you can change from carving to carving, in order to achieve many different facial expressions. (Wide nose, thin nose, big eyes, small eyes, etc.).

Using your knife tip, with the knife slanting in toward the center of the face, incise the nose/eye lines about 1/8" deep. Then, with the knife slanting toward the outside edges of the face, go over the lines again. This should release a "v" shaped sliver of wood, as seen here. The nose is starting to appear, and you have a good start on the eyes.

Using your knife, shave away a small amount of wood from both sides of the nose, and under the curved eye lines, so the nose stands out from the main face area, and the eye socket is formed.

Since the initial cheek line you drew may be now gone because of the previous step, re-establish the curved cheek line you first drew, on both sides of the nose.

Then, on both sides of the nose, and using the cheek lines you just drew, complete these lines by turning them into circles, as seen here. These will serve as rough approximations of where the full cheeks will be later, while you are working on the nose.

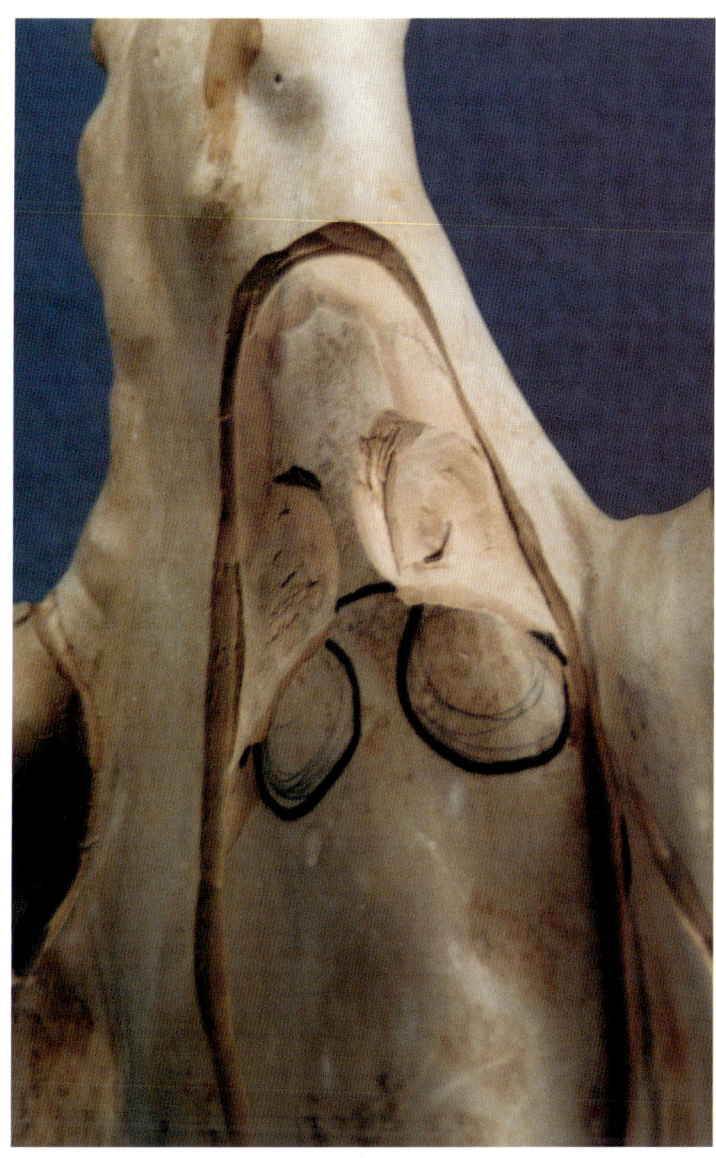

Using an in-and-up motion with your knife (a "scooping" motion), remove some wood as shown, so the upper part of the face becomes recessed from the cheek tops. This is another area you can vary from carving to carving to give different cheek effects. Round off the top edges of the cheeks, if necessary, so they blend smoothly into the upper face area.

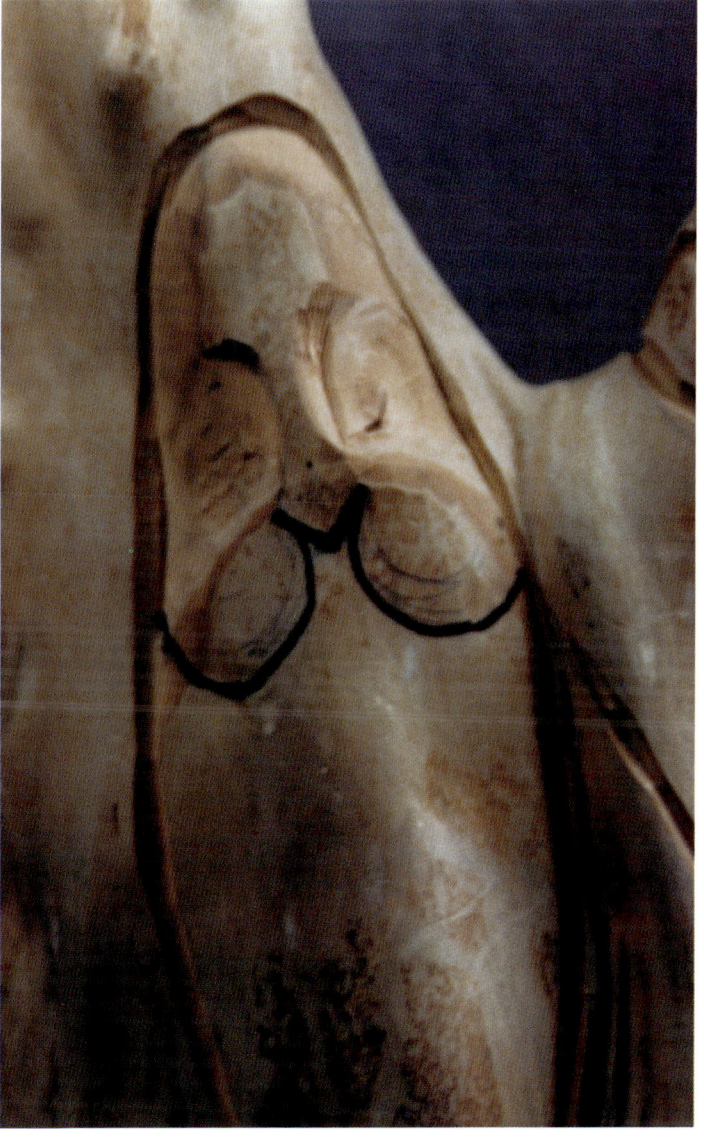

Sketch in lines to continue the cheek bottoms around and up the sides of the face. Also, sketch in the bottom of the nose. Notice that I have sketched angle lines on the nose bottom. These will be rounded off as we progress.

Using the tip of your knife, incise these lines about 1/8" deep. Then, following these lines with your knife, shave downward toward them from the top of the face, and then upward from the bottom of the face, so a "v" channel is formed. Now we have the face and nose defined, and separated from the beard.

Use your knife or #1 10 mm straight gouge to remove the sharp edges from the nose and beard where we separated them from the cheeks earlier. Also, use your knife to nip off the bottom of the nose, and round off any sharp edges that were created.

Now, sketch in the two eyes, as seen here. Yes, this is another variable you can change from one carving to the next. Are you starting to see how you could get an endless number of facial expressions by using one idea as a basic starting point?

Use your knife tip to trace over these lines, incising about 1/16" deep. Remove wood from the corners of the eyes, at about a 45 degree angle. If you incised deep enough and clean enough (here is where a dull knife will tell on you), when you make the angle cuts in the corners, the wood should just fall out.

Now, go around the edges of the eyeballs with your knife and remove a small amount of wood. This will give them a slightly rounded effect, as seen here.

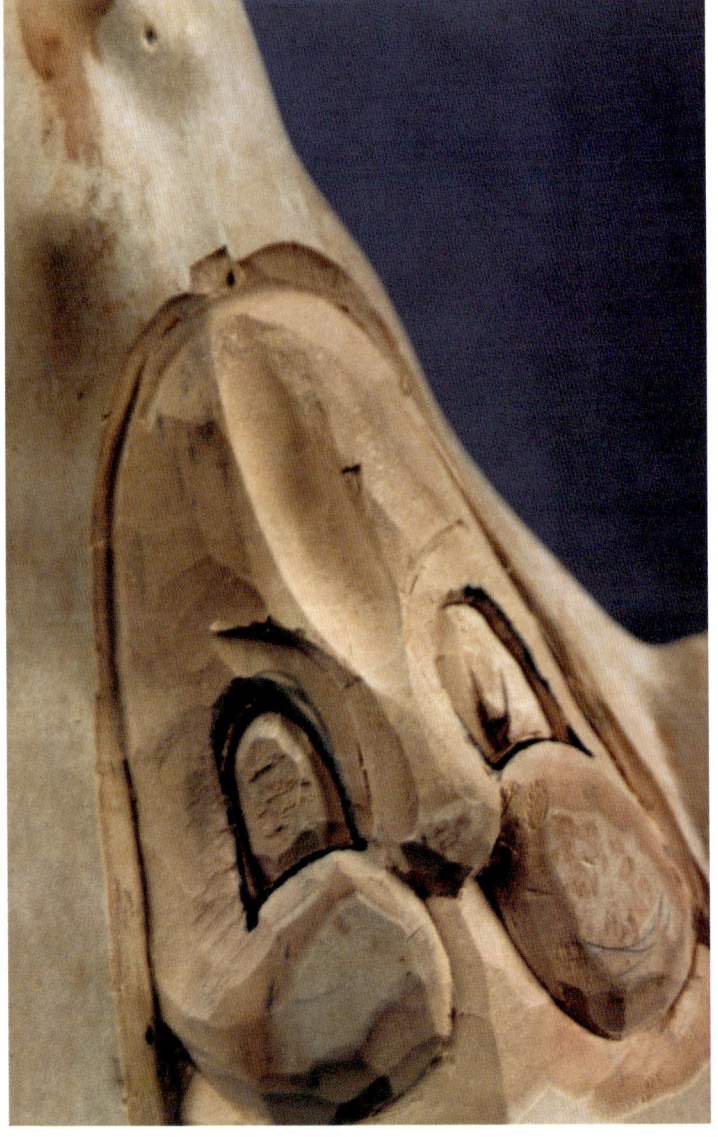

To get the eyebrows defined, first use the #9 4.5 mm "U" gouge to cut a groove up the center of the face, above the nose, centered between the eyes.

Now, with your tried-and-true scooping method, use your knife to remove some wood from the tops of the eyebrows, so they stand out from the face.

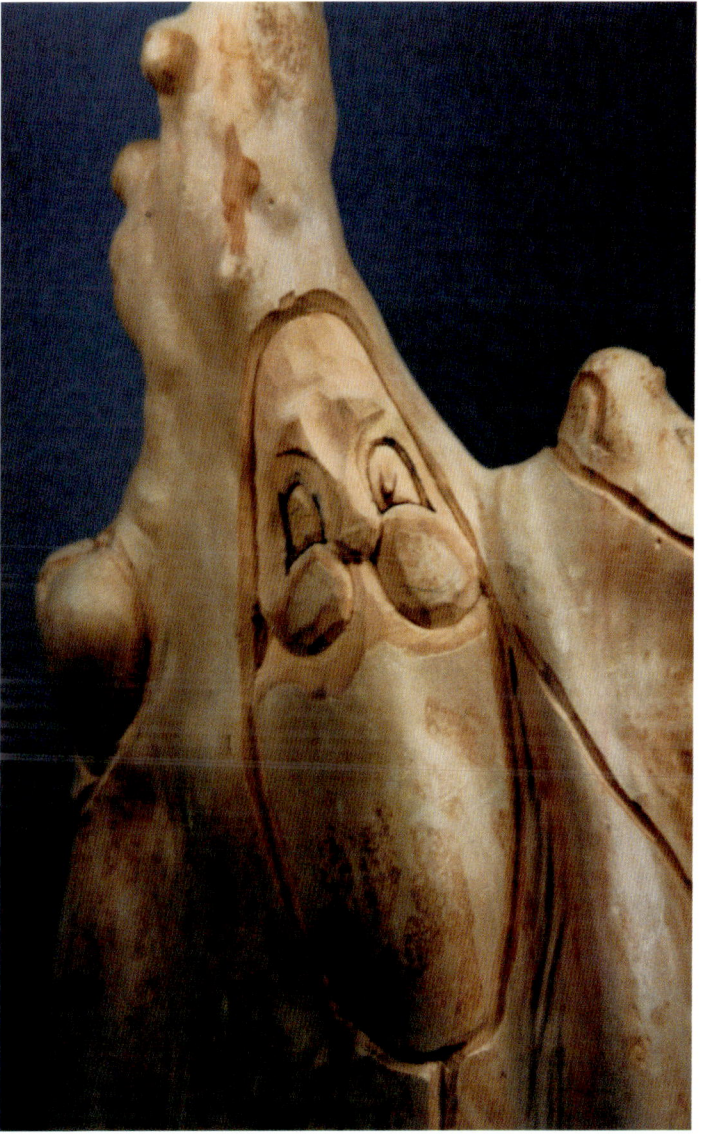

I'm happy with the main face details at this point, so I'll quit before I get into trouble, and get back to work on the beard. A good rule to live by: when you reach a point on your carving where you are satisfied, stop! Many times, when you go in and decide to "tweak" an area just a little bit more, you suddenly and sadly discover that you should have left it alone. If you don't like the way it looks, do it differently the next time.

Sketch in a curved line to define the mustache. Again, here is another variable you can change from carving to carving, so all your faces have a different "personality."

Incise the line with your knife tip about 1/8" deep. Using your knife, shave down toward the line from the top of the mustache, and up from the beard, so a "v" shaped section of wood is removed.

Now, sketch in some curved lines coming together under the nose, (but not all the way up to the nose).

Incise the lines with your knife tip about 1/8" deep. Using your knife, shave up toward the lines from below, so the wood is removed as seen here. Use your knife to round off the sharp edges on the mustache at this time.

21

Using a 1/8" nail-set, or drill bit, make a mouth hole at the inside top of the mustache.

Sketch in the lower lip. (*Another variable!*)

Incise the lip lines about 1/16" deep with your knife tip, then shave away a small amount of wood below the lines, in order to make the lip stand out.

Nip off the bottom point of the lip with your knife, round off the sharp edges, and the lip is done.

Use the 10 mm straight gouge to remove wood from the robe so the lower part of the beard stands out.

Use the #9 4.5 mm "U" gouge and #9 6 mm "U" gouge to add details to the mustache, beard, and hair. For extra effect (optional), you can then use the #39 4.5 mm "V" gouge to cut a few more details into the beard. You may be bold and daring and also use a gouge to add texture to the eyebrows. If you don't do this, your Santa will still look just fine.

Use your knife to remove wood from the left mitten near the sleeve, so it appears to be coming out of the sleeve. I have also removed excess wood from this mitten area to bring it more into proportion with the size of the right mitten.

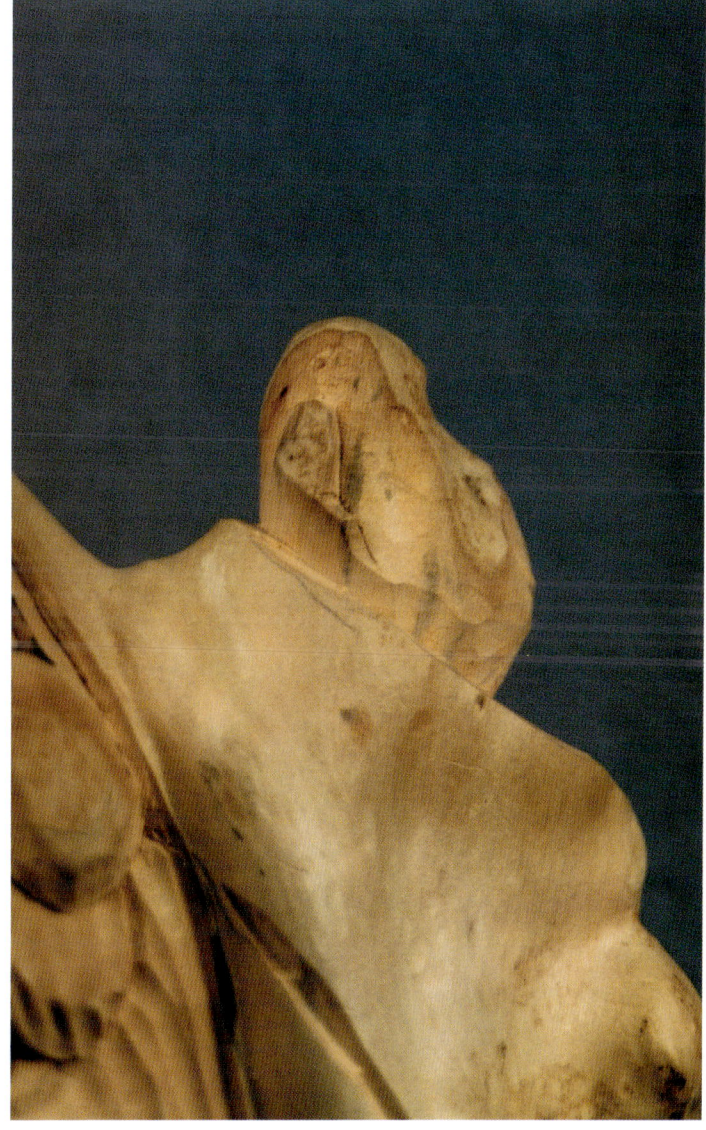

Use your knife to remove some wood from the upper part of the left mitten so the thumb stands out. Round off any sharp edges on the thumb.

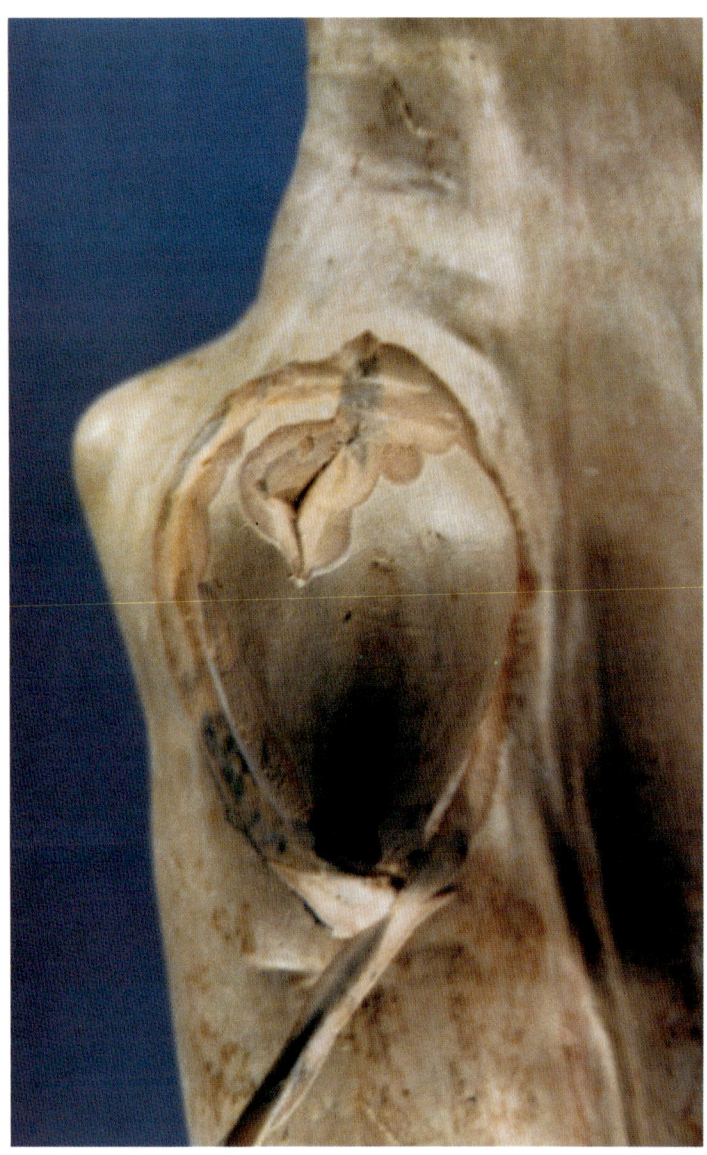

Repeat these last two steps in order to get the right mitten carved.

Use your knife and a 10 mm straight gouge to remove wood from the robe area so the left arm and sleeve stands out from the body.

Repeat this procedure for the right arm.

Add texture to the "fur" using the 6 mm "U" gouge.

This completes the carving of the large wood spirit Santa. Now, we'll go through the steps of carving an icicle Santa, which you can use as an ornament, then we'll paint both pieces.

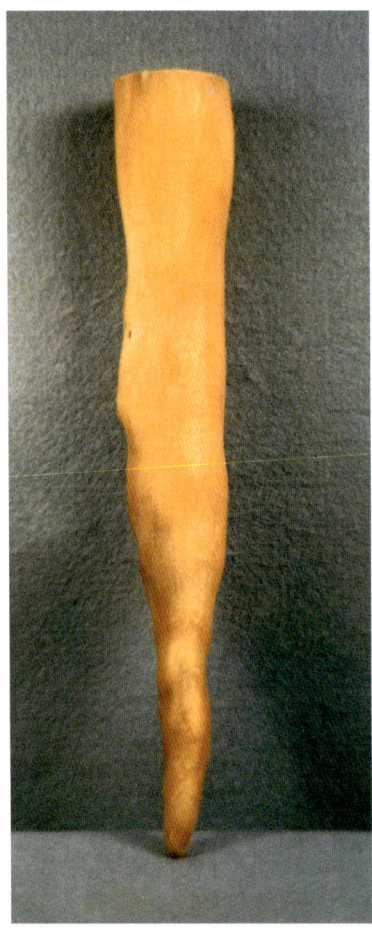

This is the cypress knee I chose for the icicle Santa ornament. We will carve this one with the pointed end down, so it will resemble an icicle when we are done, thus the name "icicle" Santa.

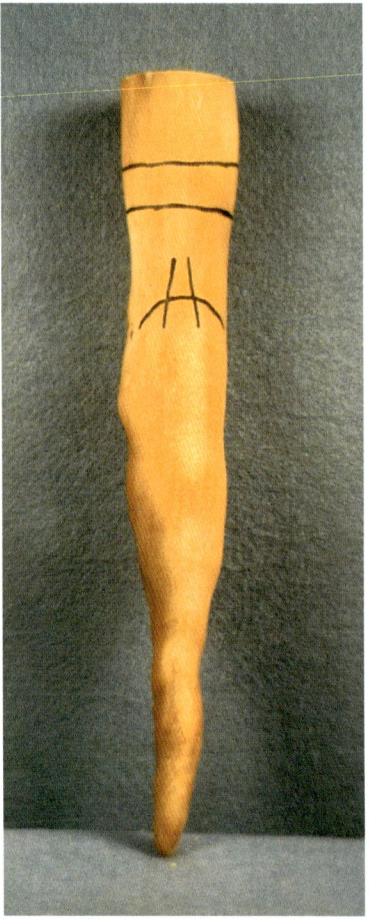

Here are some rough-in lines I sketched with a marker pen, just for a reference. Again, if you saw a different spot where you would have placed the lines, that's fine, also.

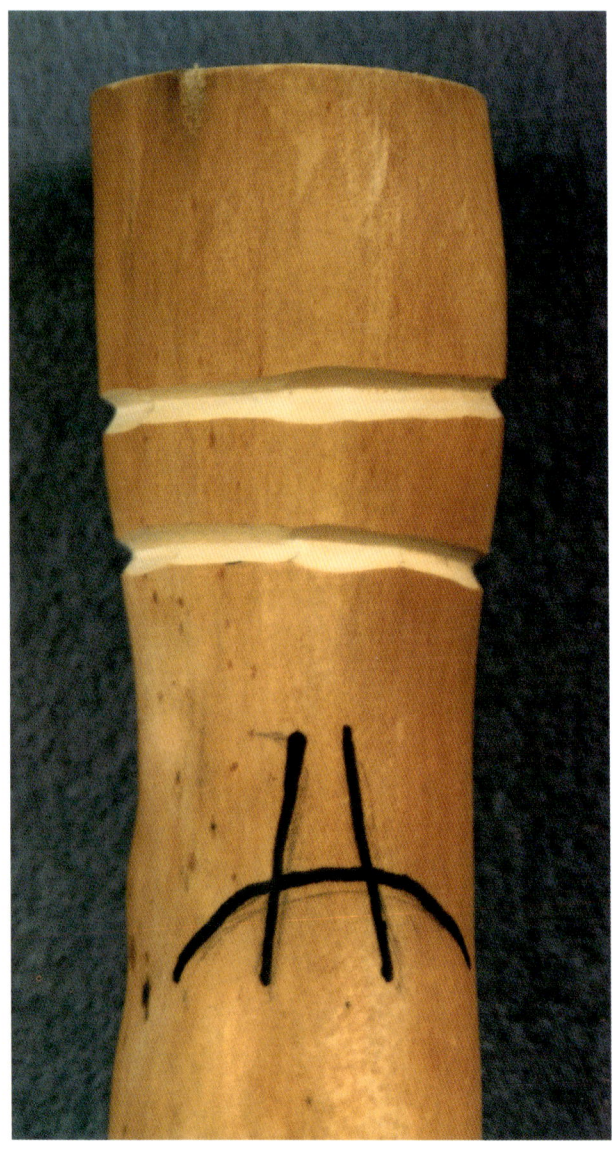

Use the 4.5 mm "V" gouge to trace over the two lines which go around the top of the icicle.

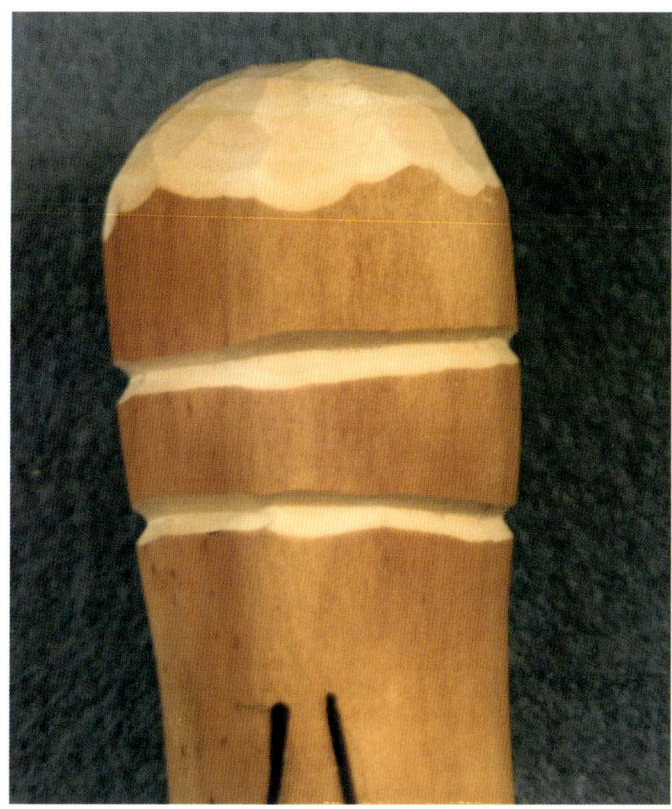

Round off the top of the hat with your knife.

Round off the lower half of the top part of the hat, so it flows into the band which will become "fur" later.

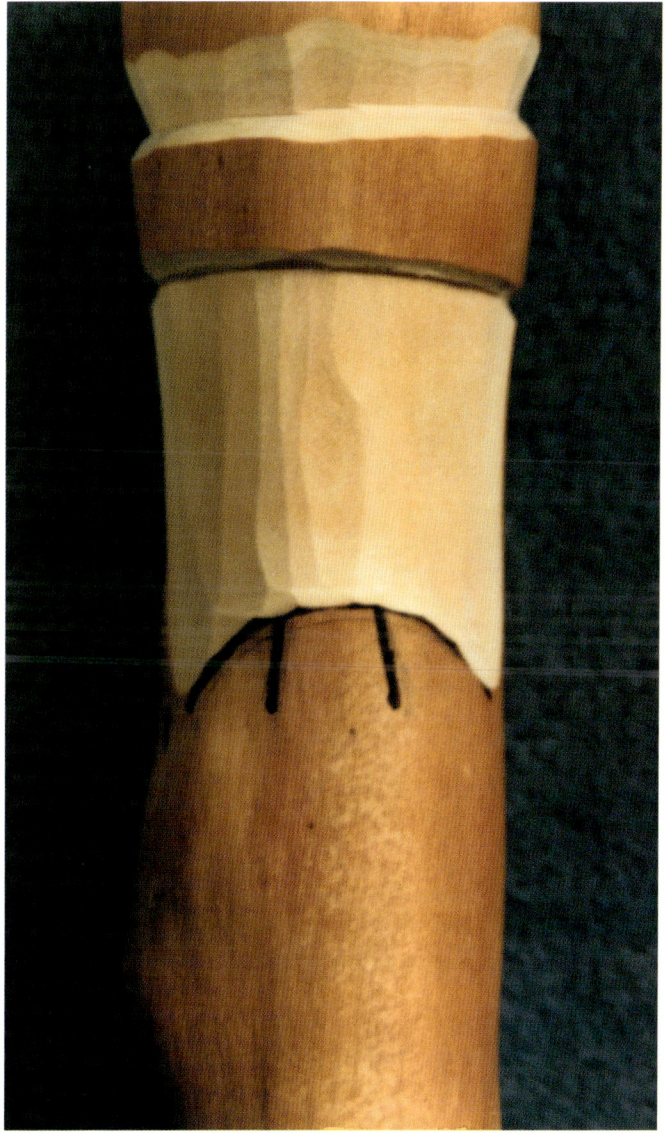

Using your knife, scoop away wood above the curved line so the cheek area will stand out from the face.

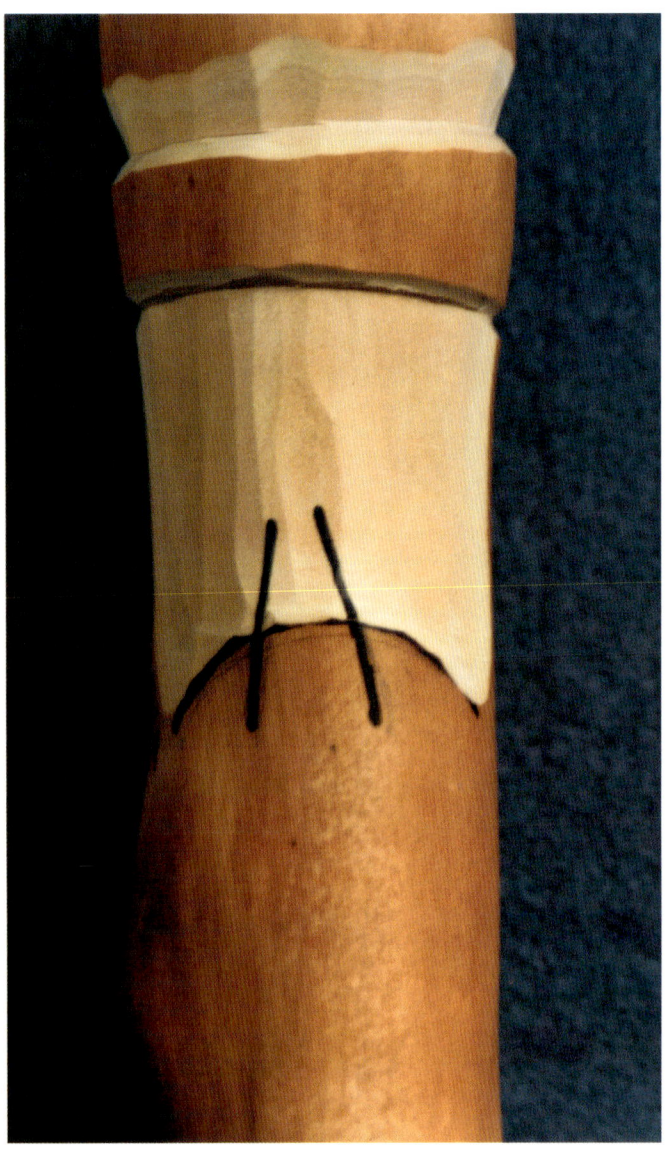

Sketch the nose lines back in place.

Using your knife, incise the nose lines about 1/8" deep. Remove wood from both sides of the nose to separate it and define it from the cheeks (as you did on the large carving).

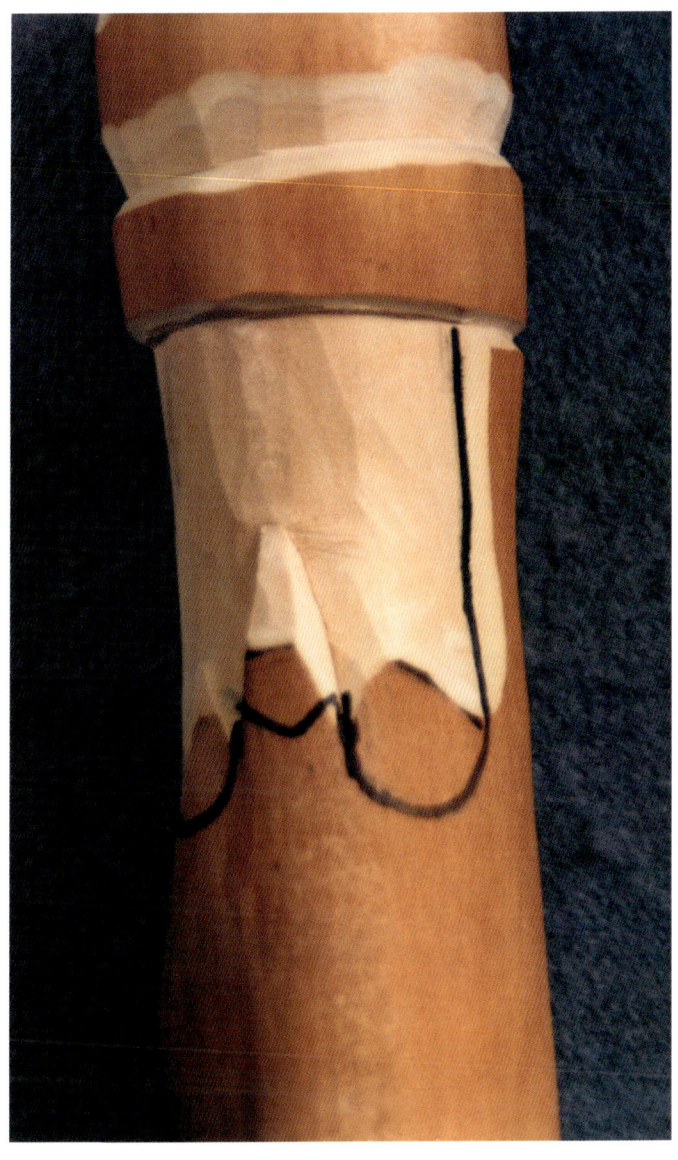

Sketch lines to define the cheeks and bottom of the nose.

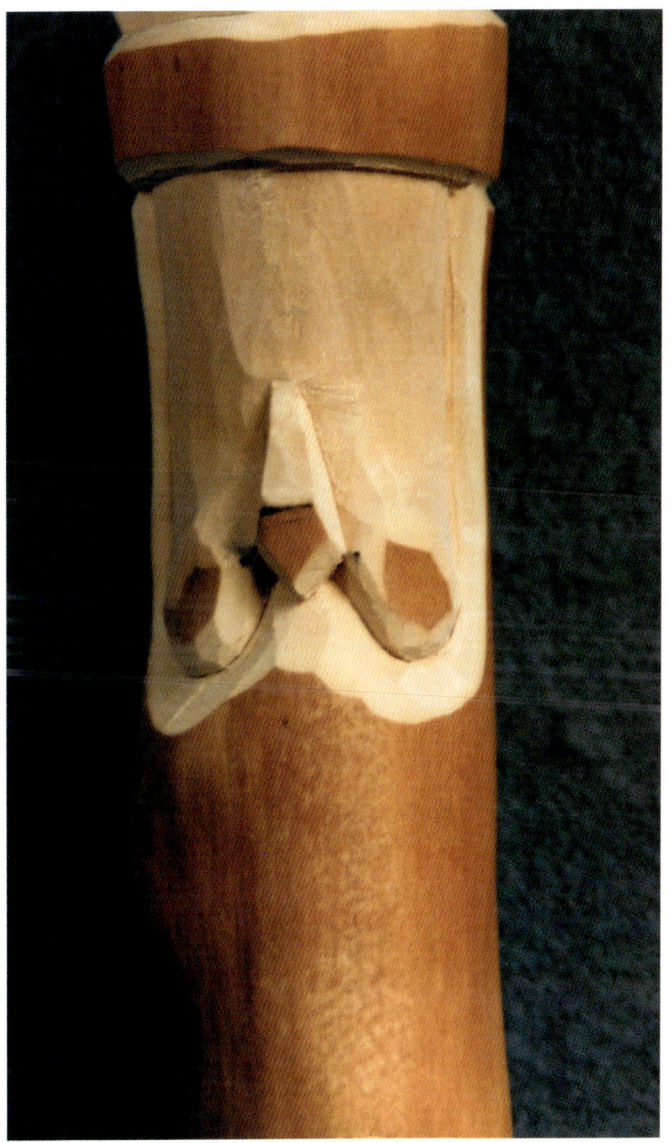

Incise the lines about 1/8" deep with your knife. Shave down toward the incision, and up toward the incision, to form a "v" channel. This separates and defines the cheeks, face, and bottom of the nose.

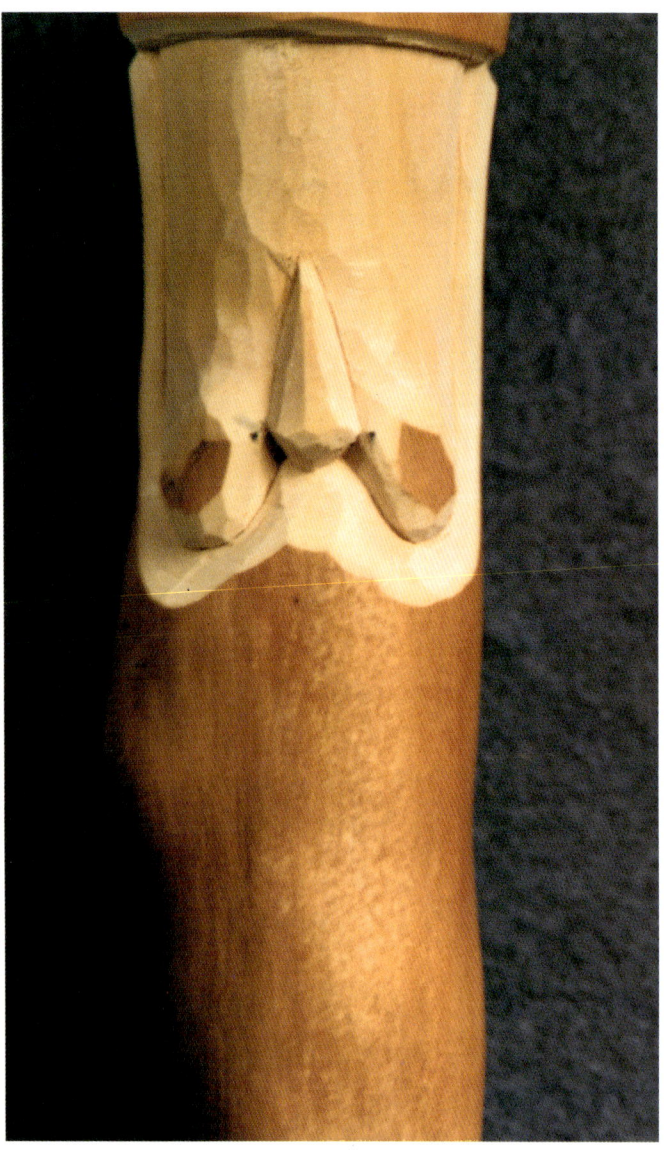

Using your knife, round off the sharp edges of the nose.

Use your knife to remove wood just below the band on the hat, so the hair will appear to be flowing into the bottom of the hat.

Sketch in the two eyes, similar to the way you did on the other project.

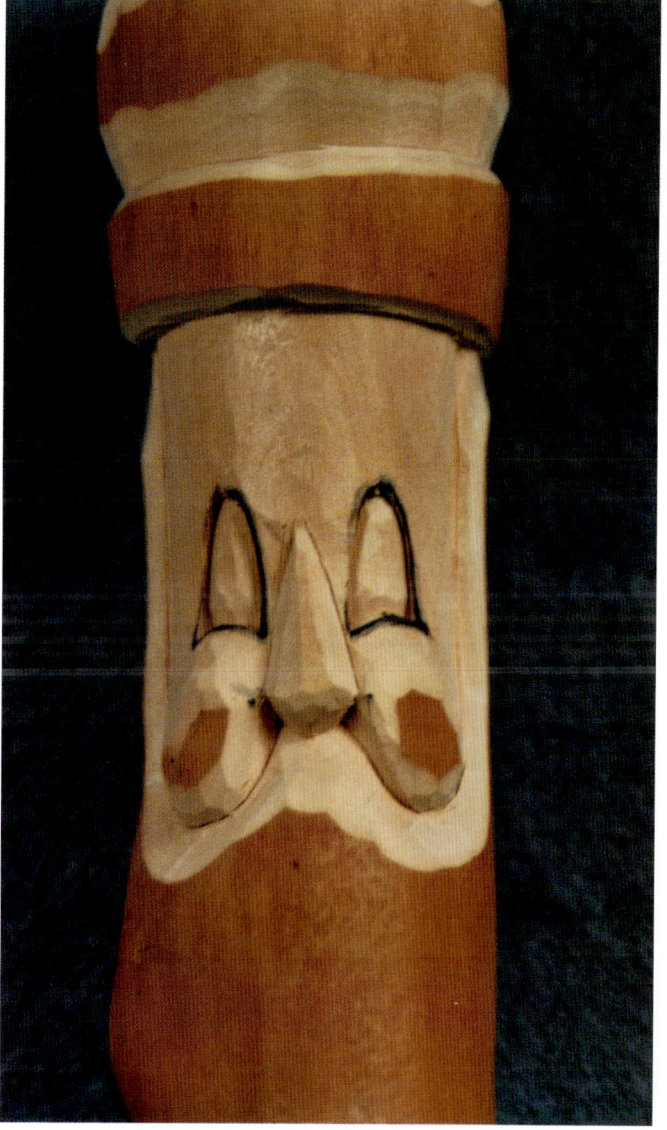

Incise the eyes about 1/8" deep, and remove wood from the corners and around the eyeball, as we did on the other project.

Use the 6 mm "U" gouge to remove wood from between the eyes.

Again, as before, scoop away wood from above the eyes, to form the eyebrows.

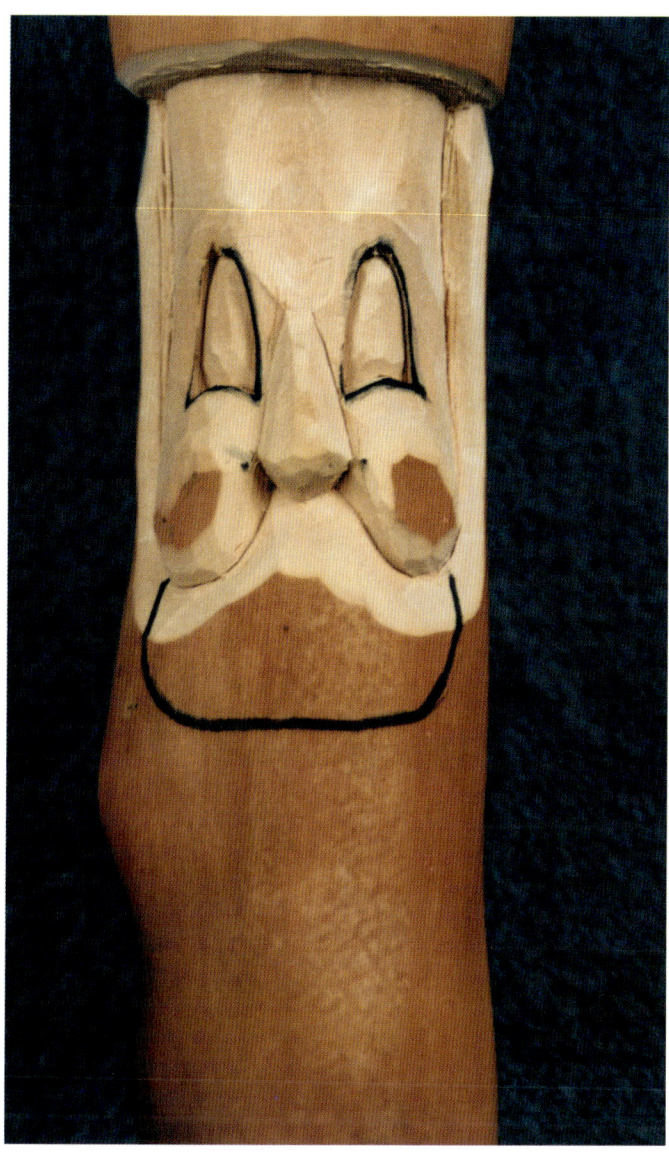

Sketch in the mustache outline.

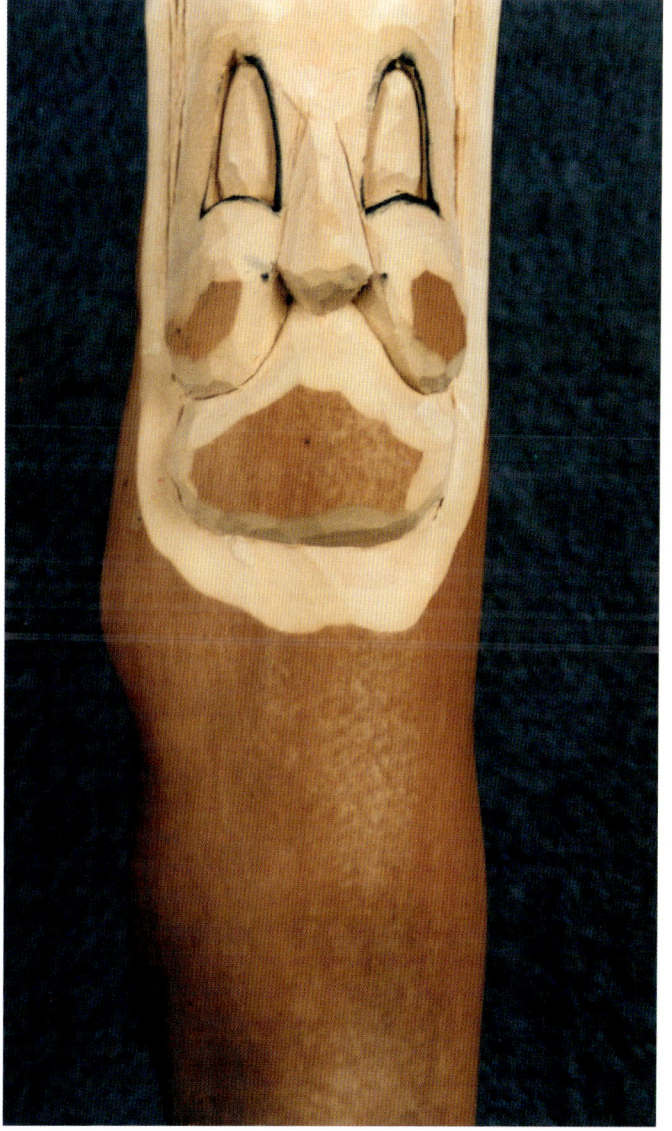

As before, incise the line, then remove wood using your knife to form a "v" channel.

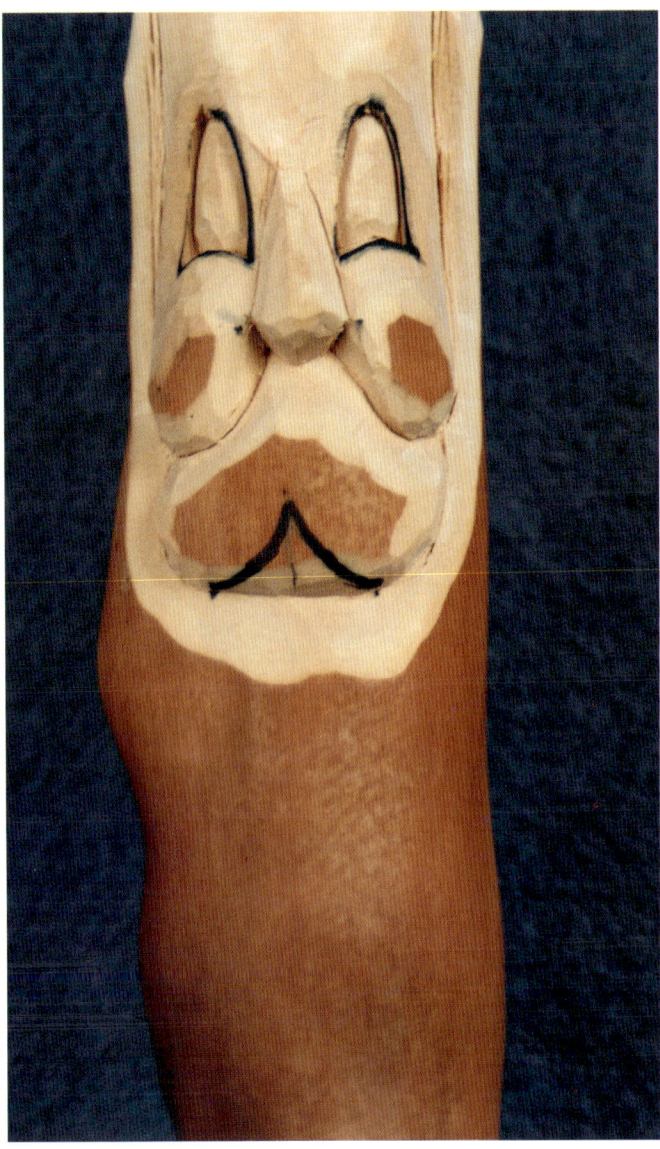

Sketch in the curved lines at the bottom center of the mustache.

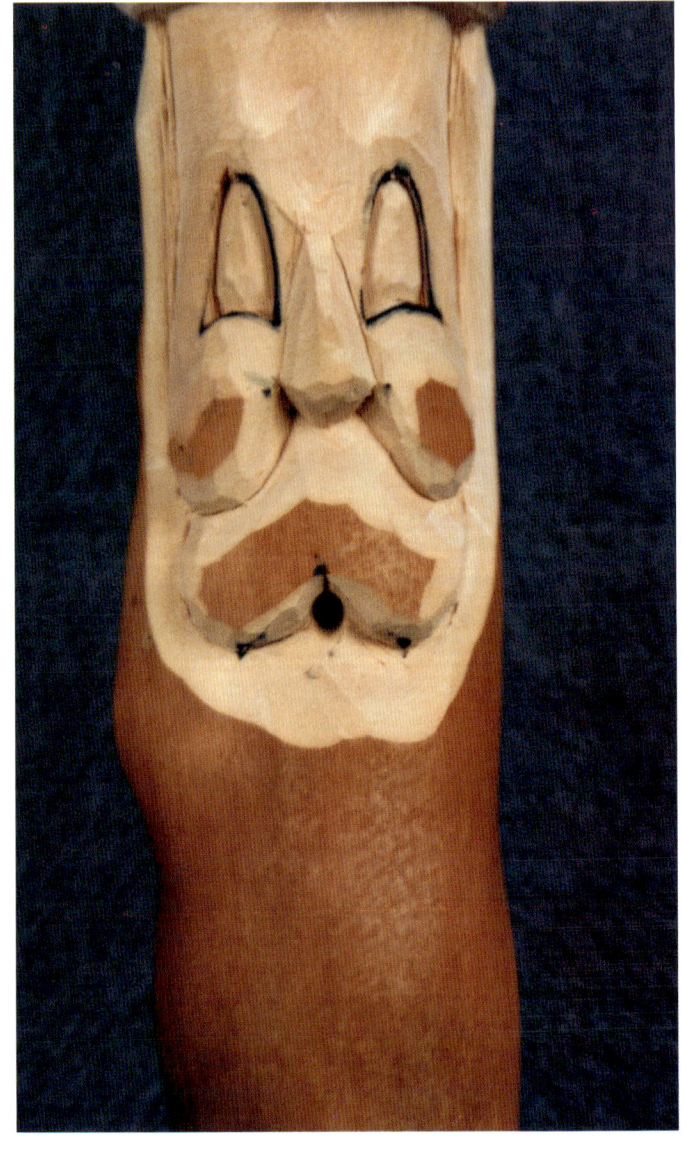

Remove the wood using your knife, and make the mouth hole.

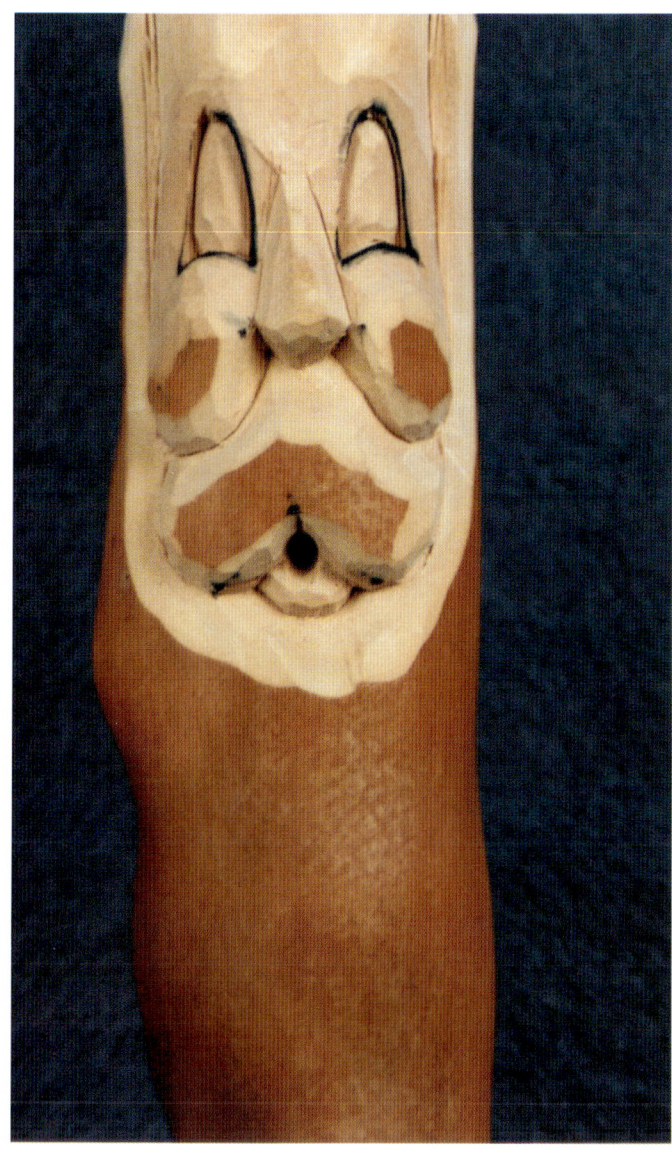

Carve the lower lip as we did on the previous project.

Add texture to the "fur" around the hat using the 6 mm "U" gouge.

Use the 4.5 mm "U" gouge and the 6 mm "U" gouge to add texture to the mustache and beard. The 4.5 mm "V" gouge may also be used to add additional texture effects.

Last, add a screw eye hook to the top of the hat, so the ornament can hang from the tree next Christmas.

Guess what? Both projects are done as far as the carving is concerned!! I'm going to take a slight break, then I'll take you through the painting of both projects.

Painting the Projects

Painting the Large Santa

The face and lip is Flesh. While the paint is still damp, blend some Blush Flesh onto the cheeks, tip of the nose, and lip. This will give ol' Santa a wind-burned look.

Paint the eyeballs, eyebrows, and beard White. When the White of the eyes is dry, paint a section of each eye Country Blue. When that is dry, paint a smaller section of each eye Black. Finally, add a White highlight to each eye to give Santa the "spark of life."

The mittens are Black.

The fur is Light Buttermilk.

The robe is Santa Red.

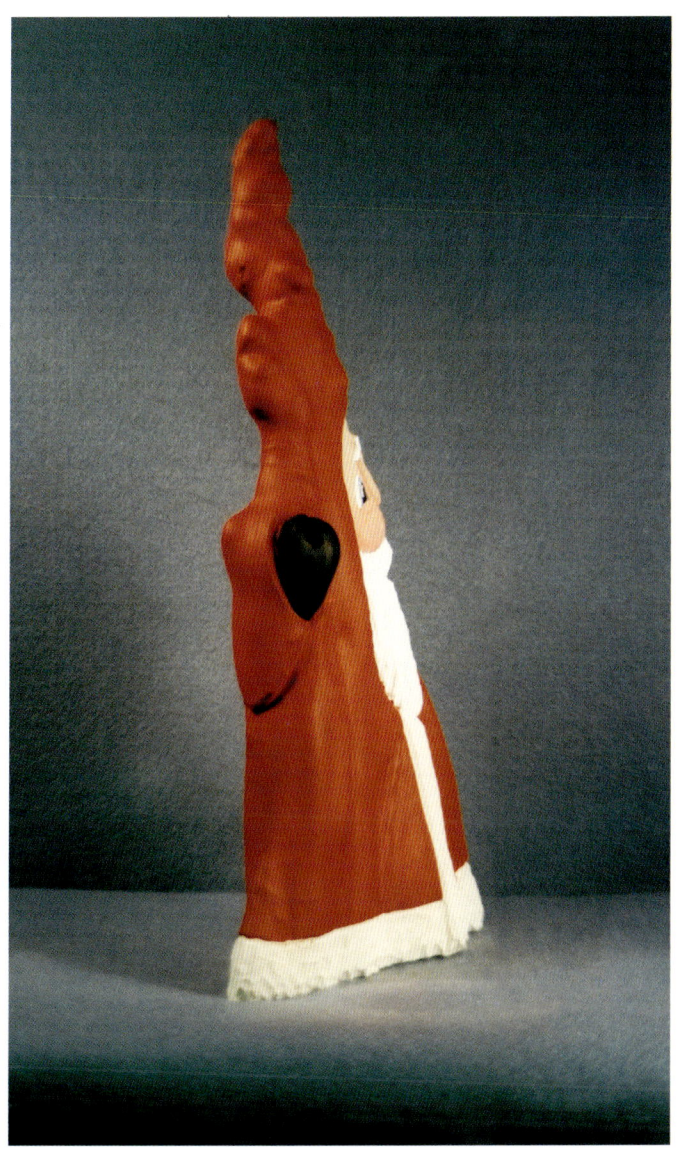

Finished large Santa - right side view.

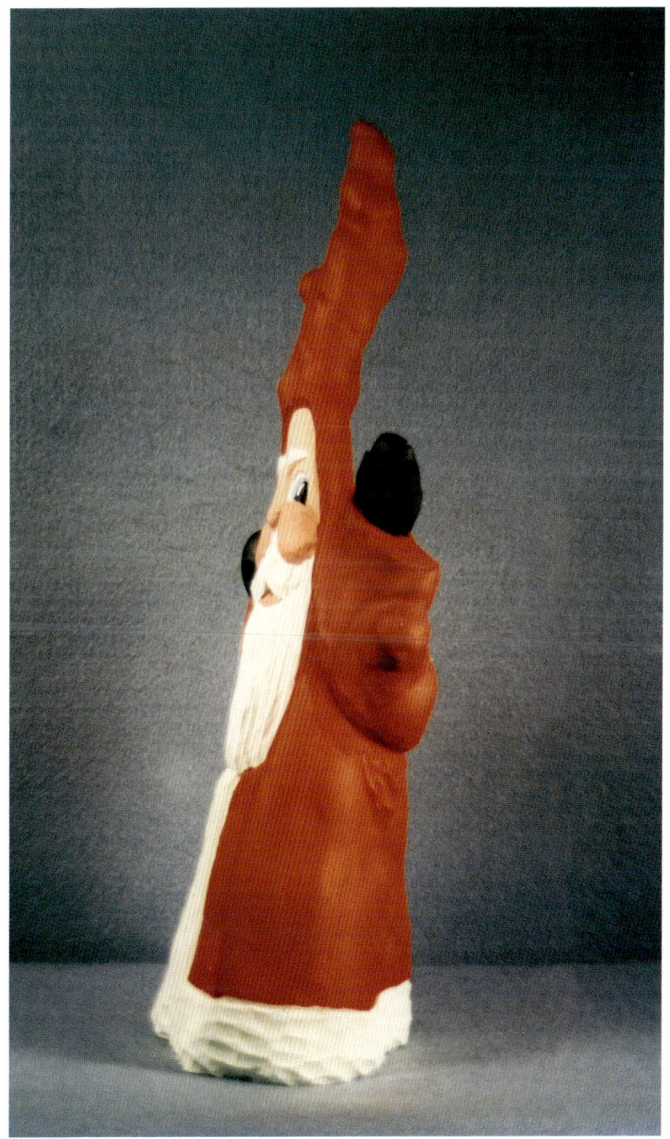

Finished large Santa - left side view.

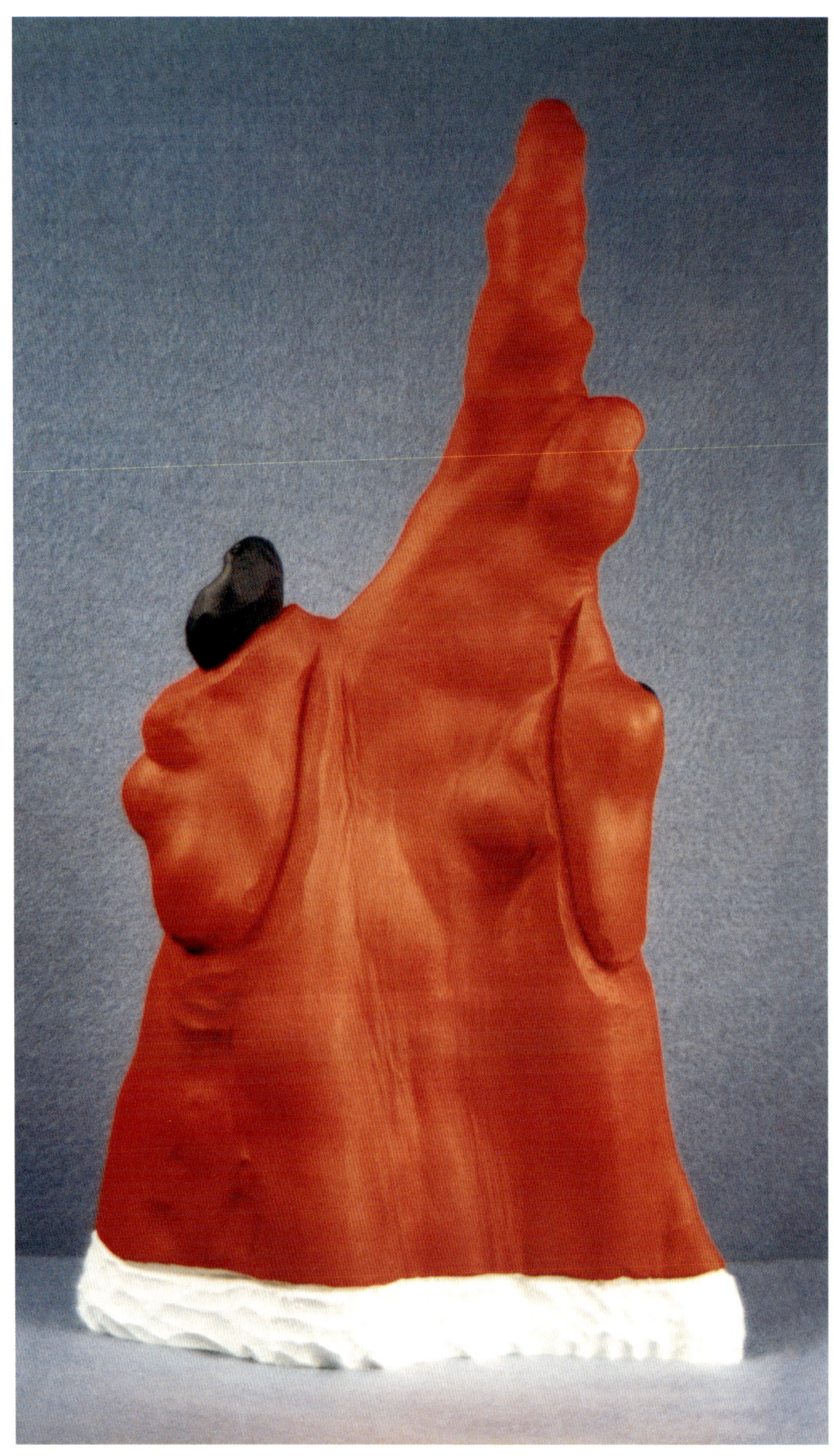

Finished large Santa - rear view.

Painting the Icicle Santa

Paint the face and beard using the same methods used in painting the large Santa.

The fur on the hat is Light Buttermilk, and the top of the hat is Santa Red.

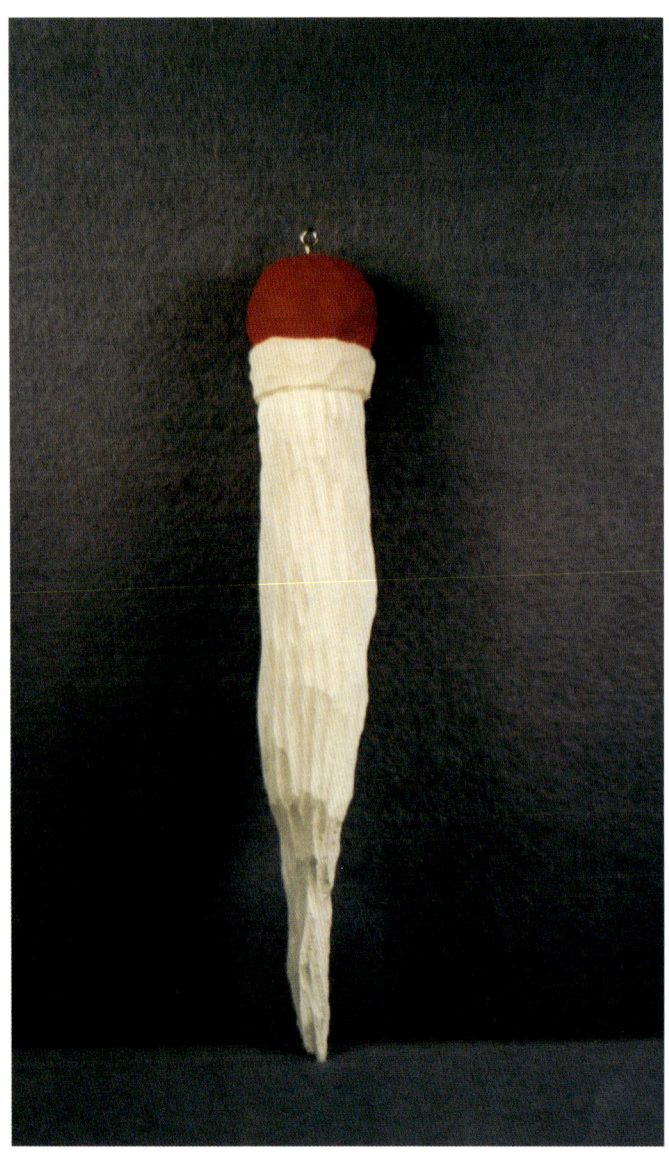

Completed icicle - rear view.

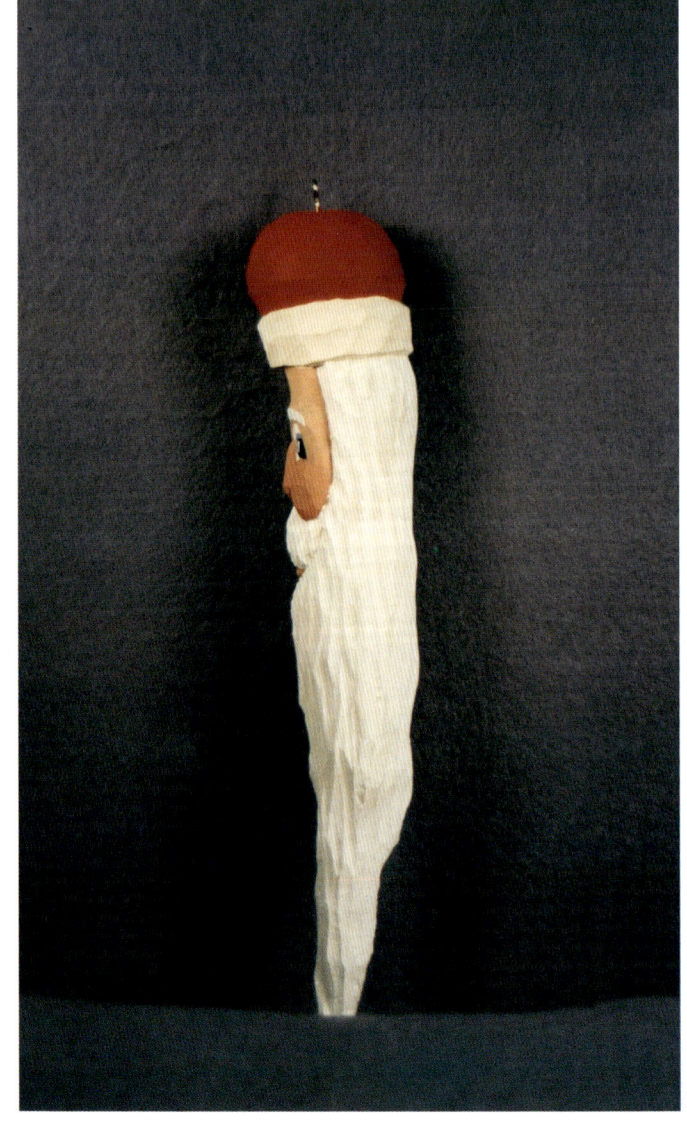

Completed icicle - side view.

For future posterity, you should sign, number, and date your carving. This makes it more valuable to the collectors who will be seeking out your work some day, if not already. I hope that in some way I have been able to help each of you with some aspect of carving and painting. When we share tips and information, we all become better carvers. If you have any comments or questions about something in this book, or if you have an idea you'd like to see me put in a future book, please feel free to write, e-mail, or call me at the following address and telephone number. I welcome any comments or suggestions you have.

Al Streetman
402 North Broad Street
Guthrie, Oklahoma 73044
(405) 282-8234
astreetman@mmcable.com

Gallery and Study Models

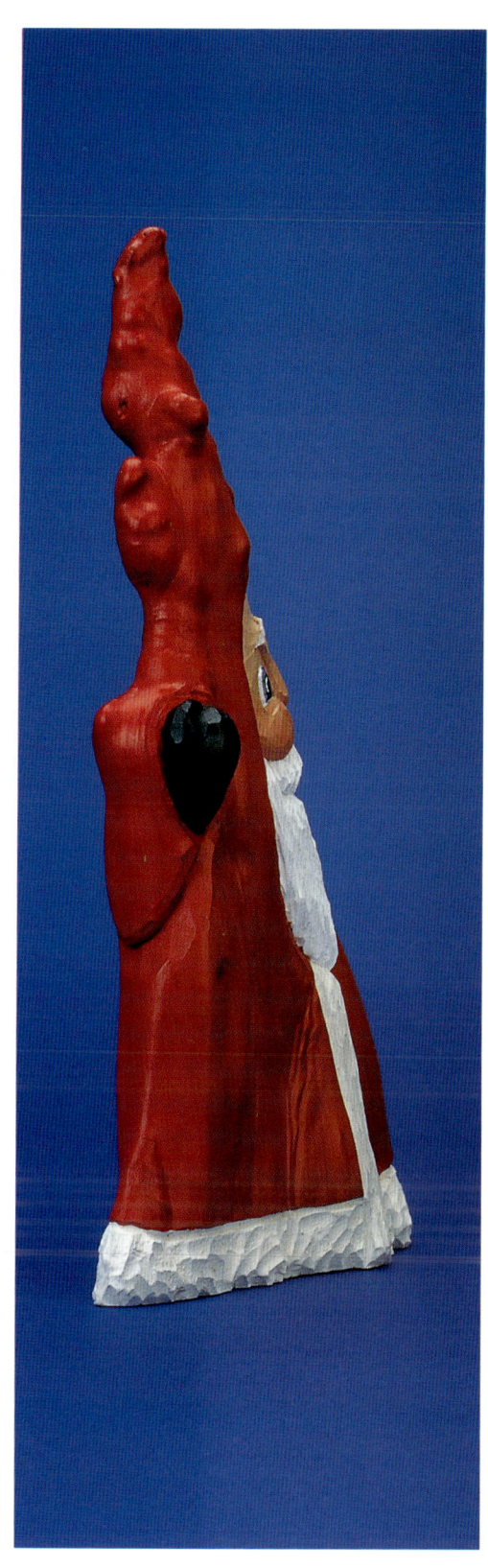

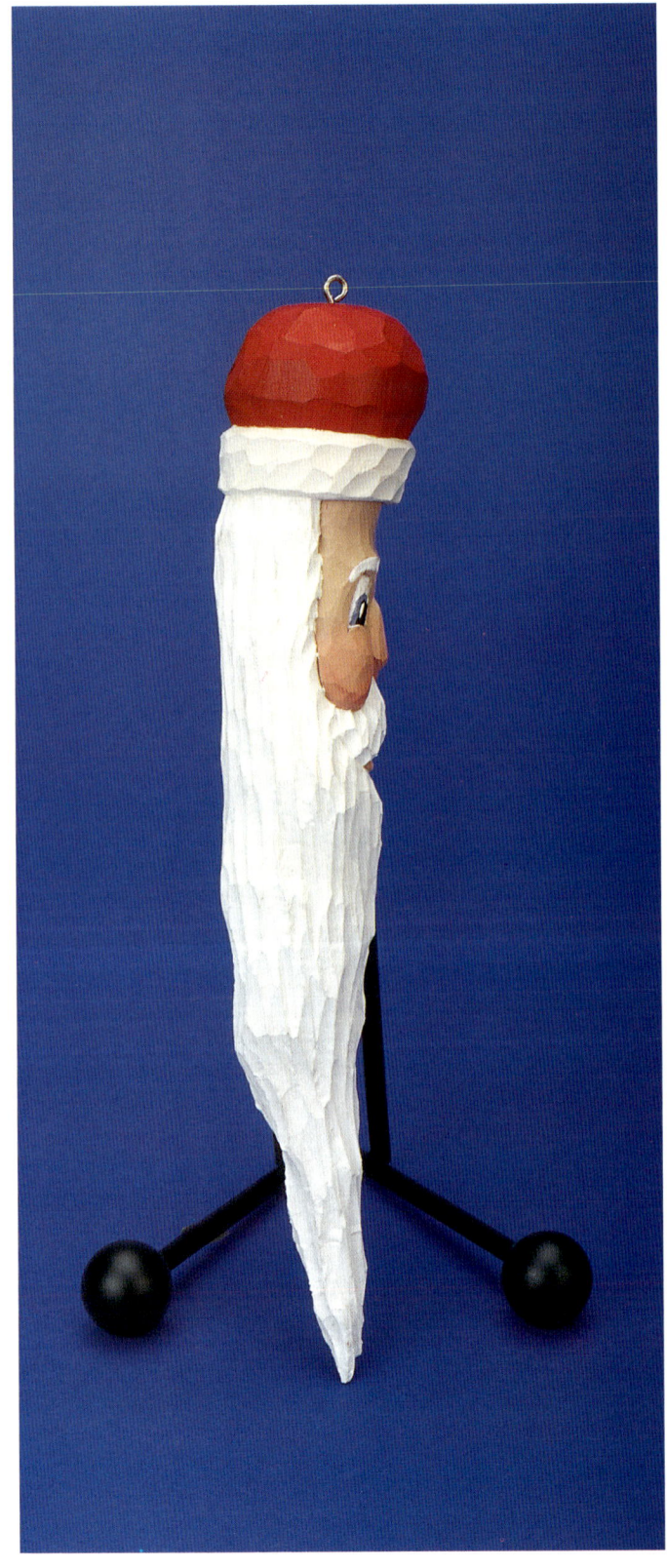

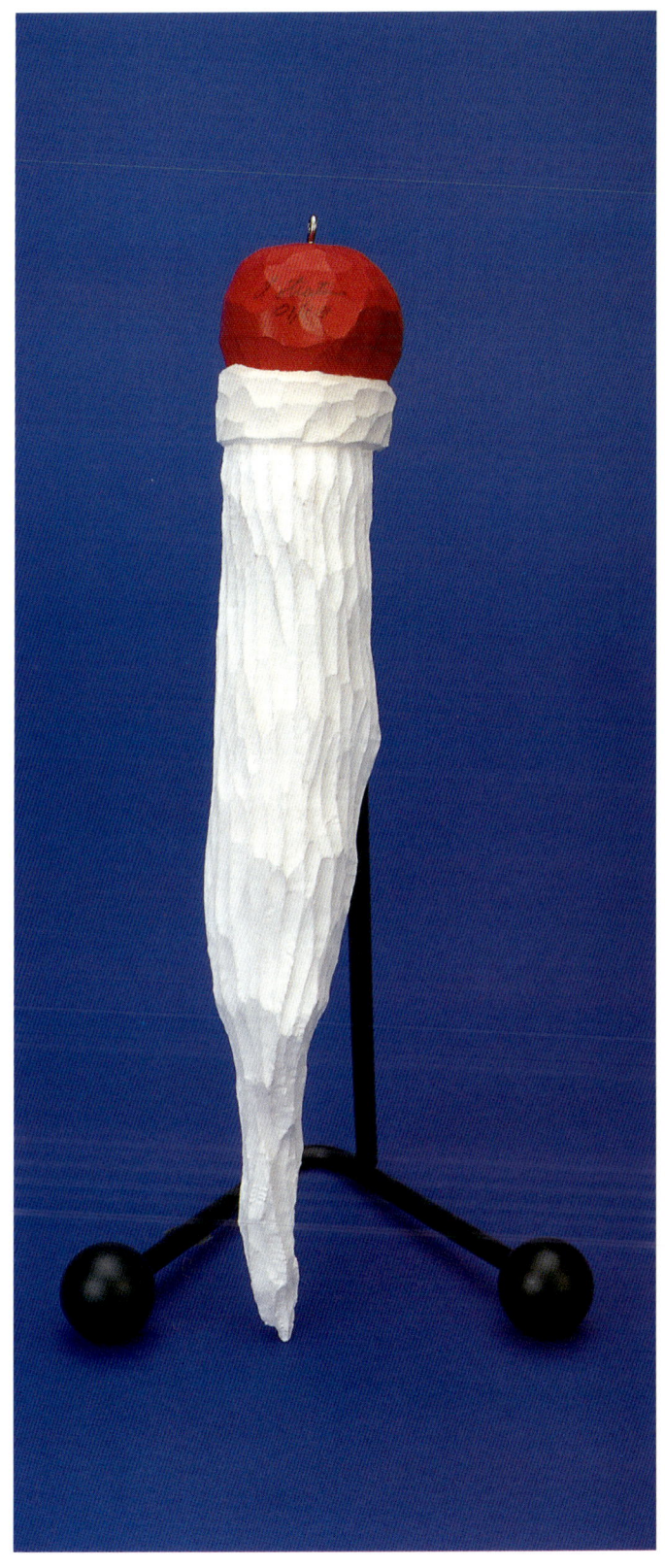

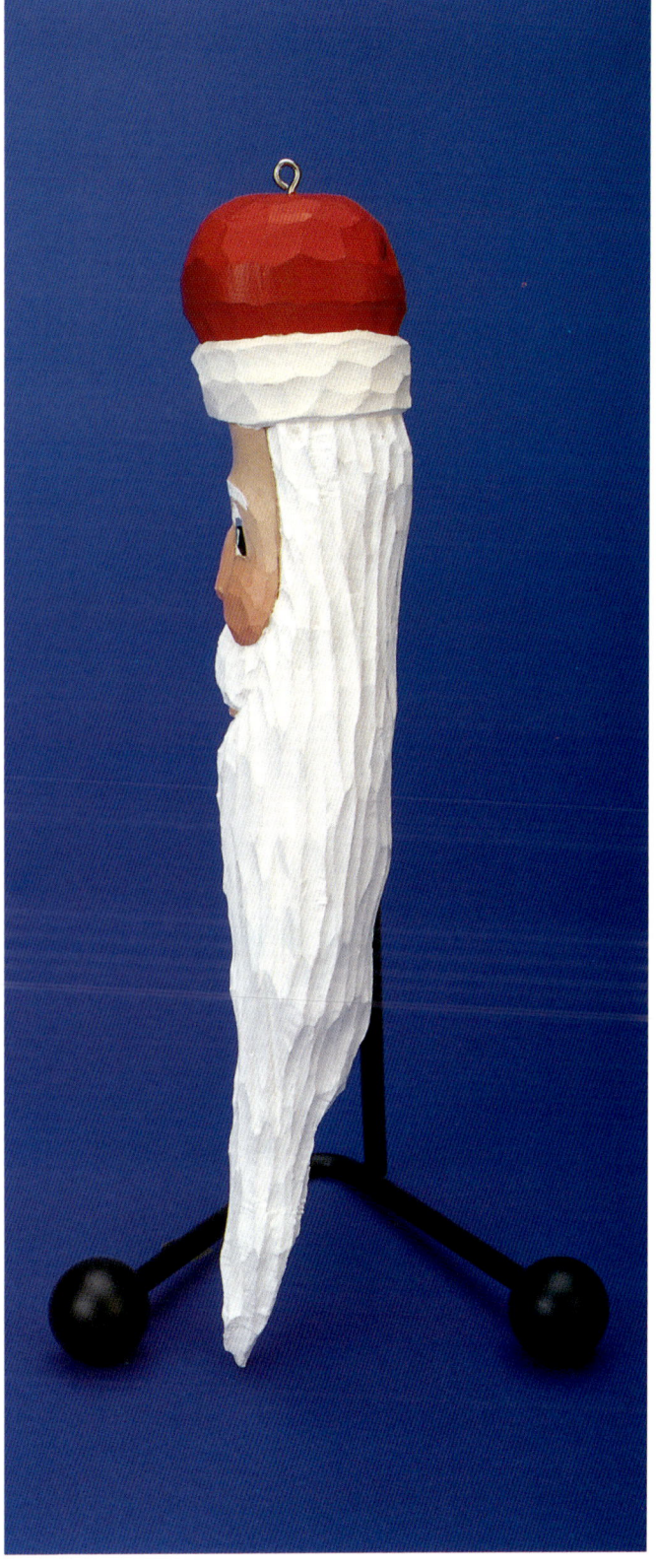

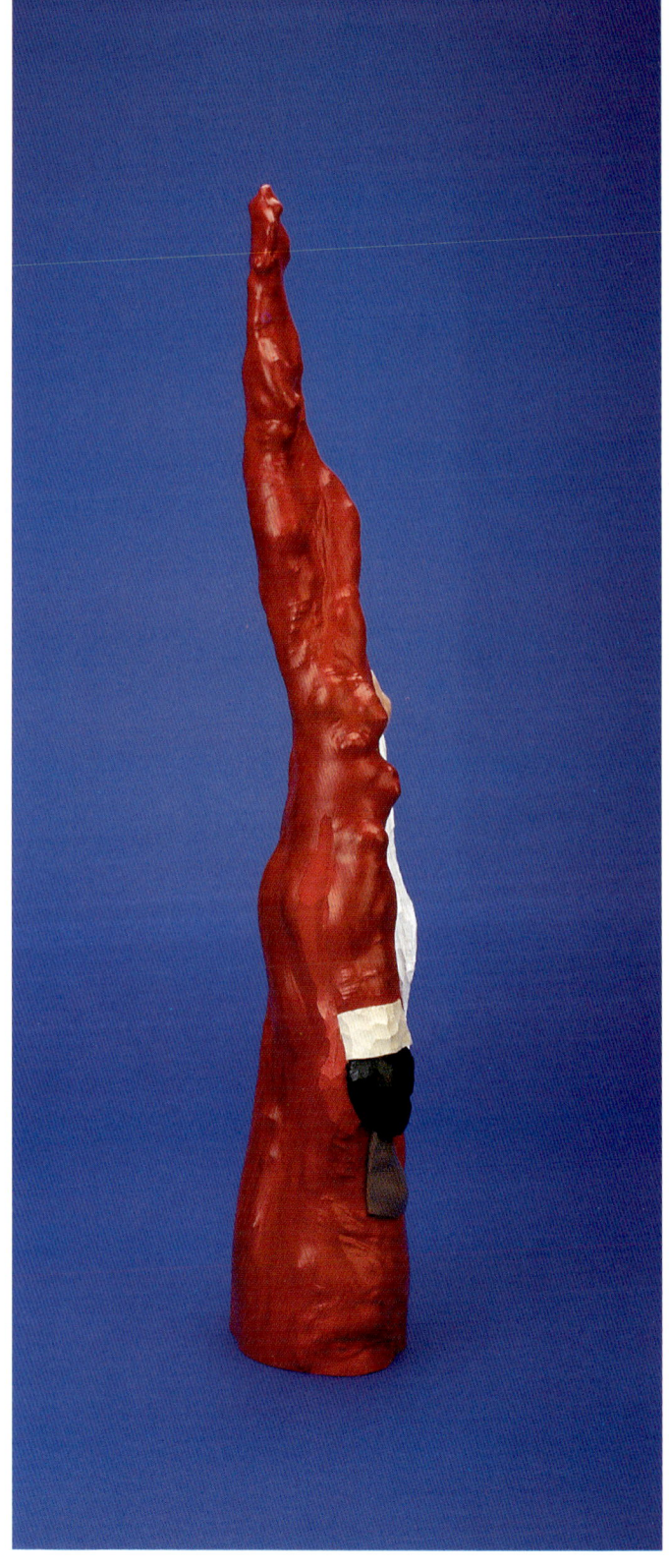

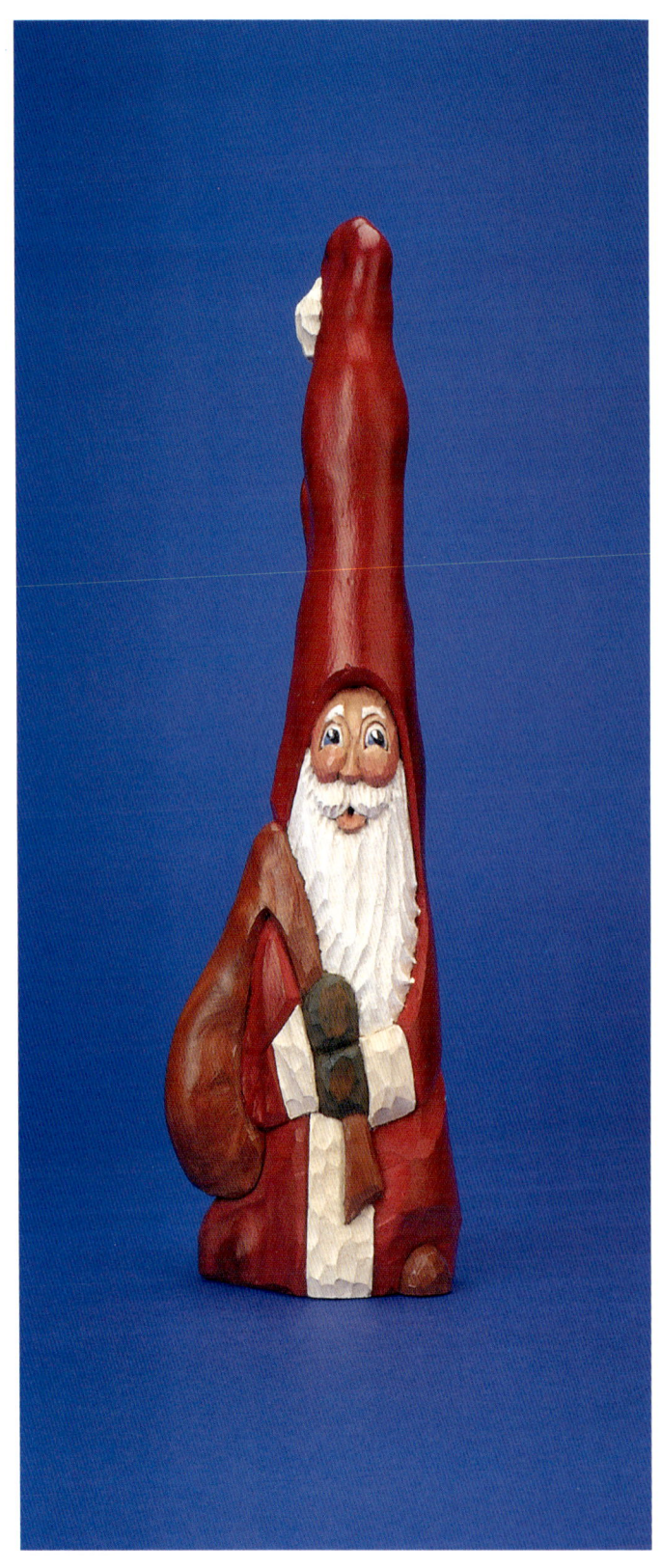

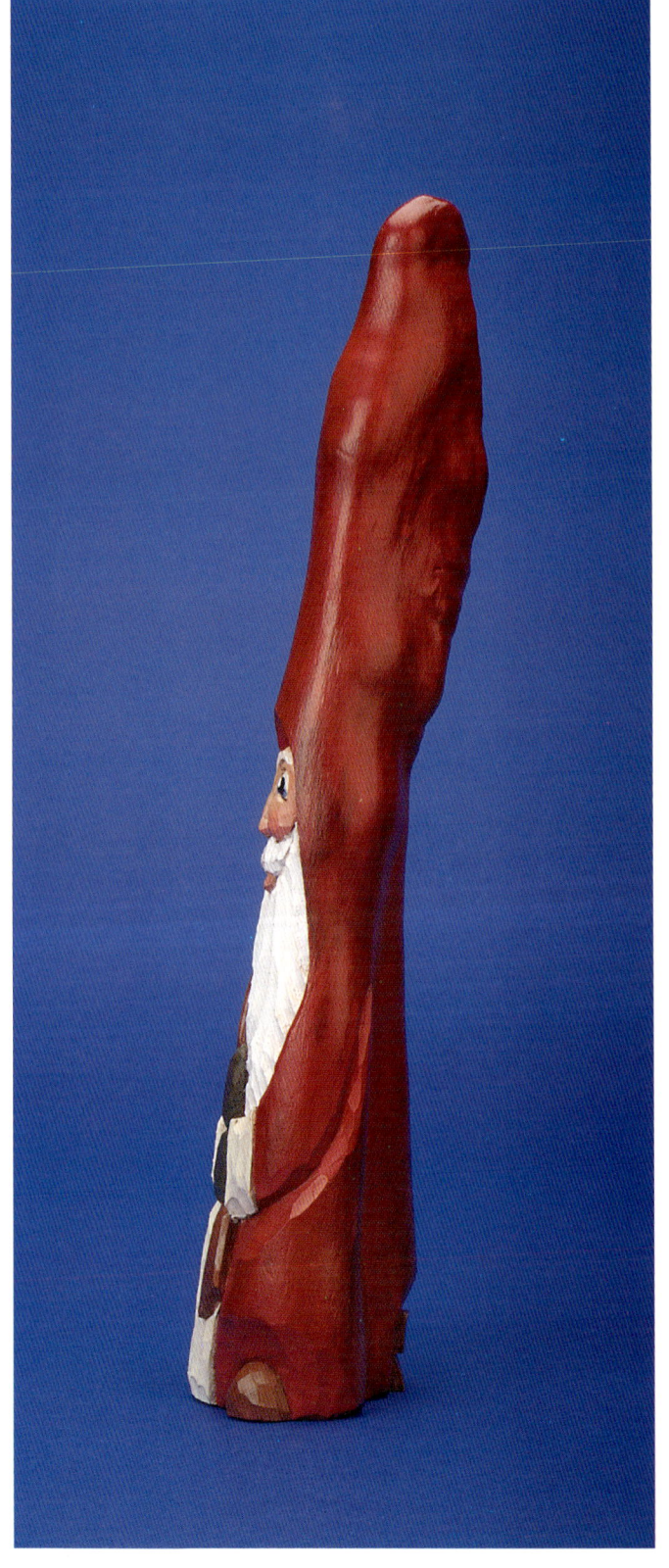

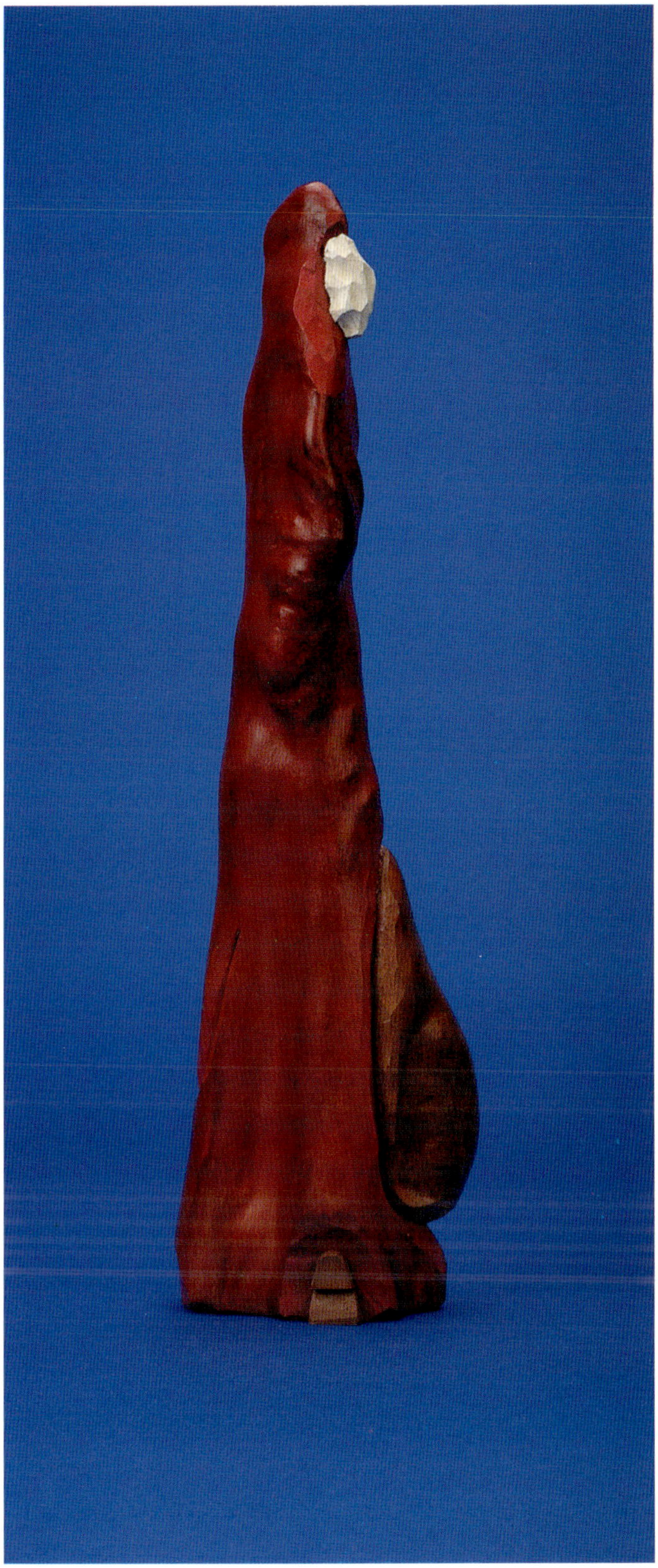

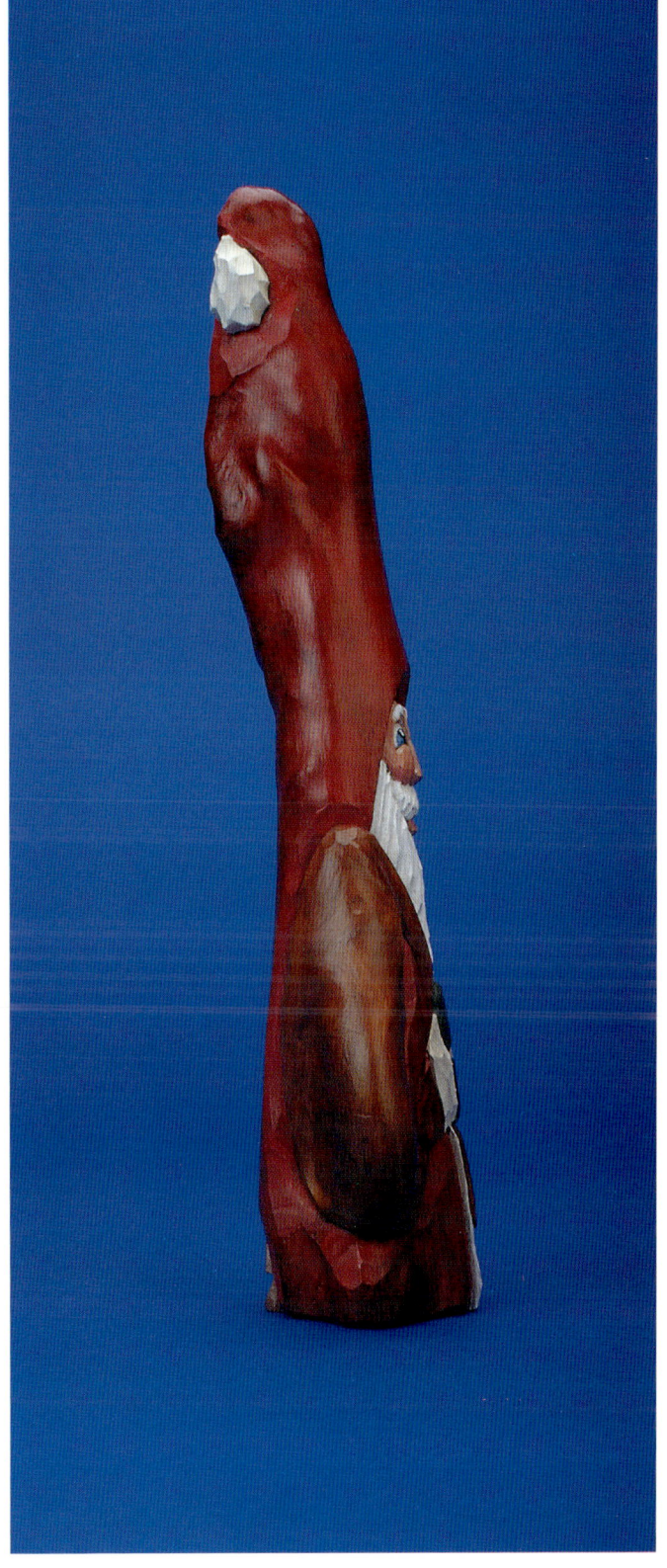

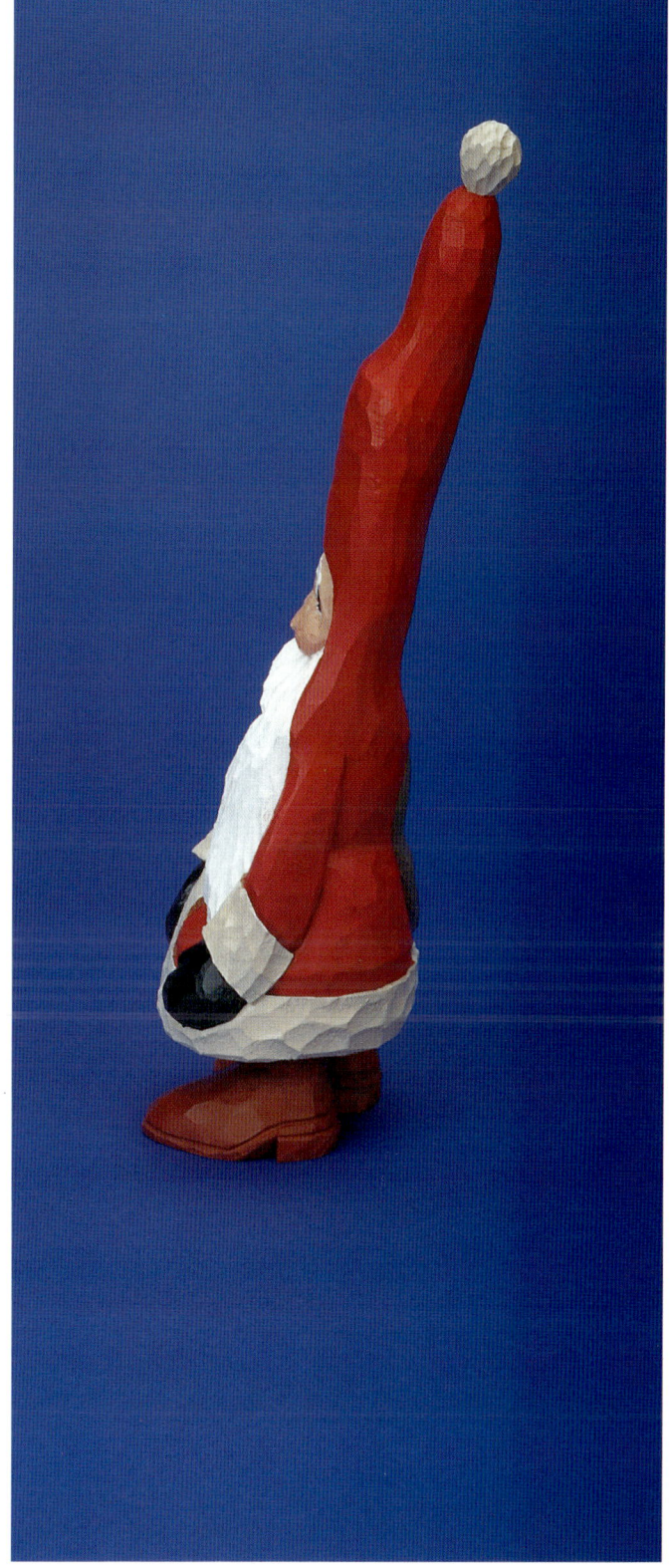

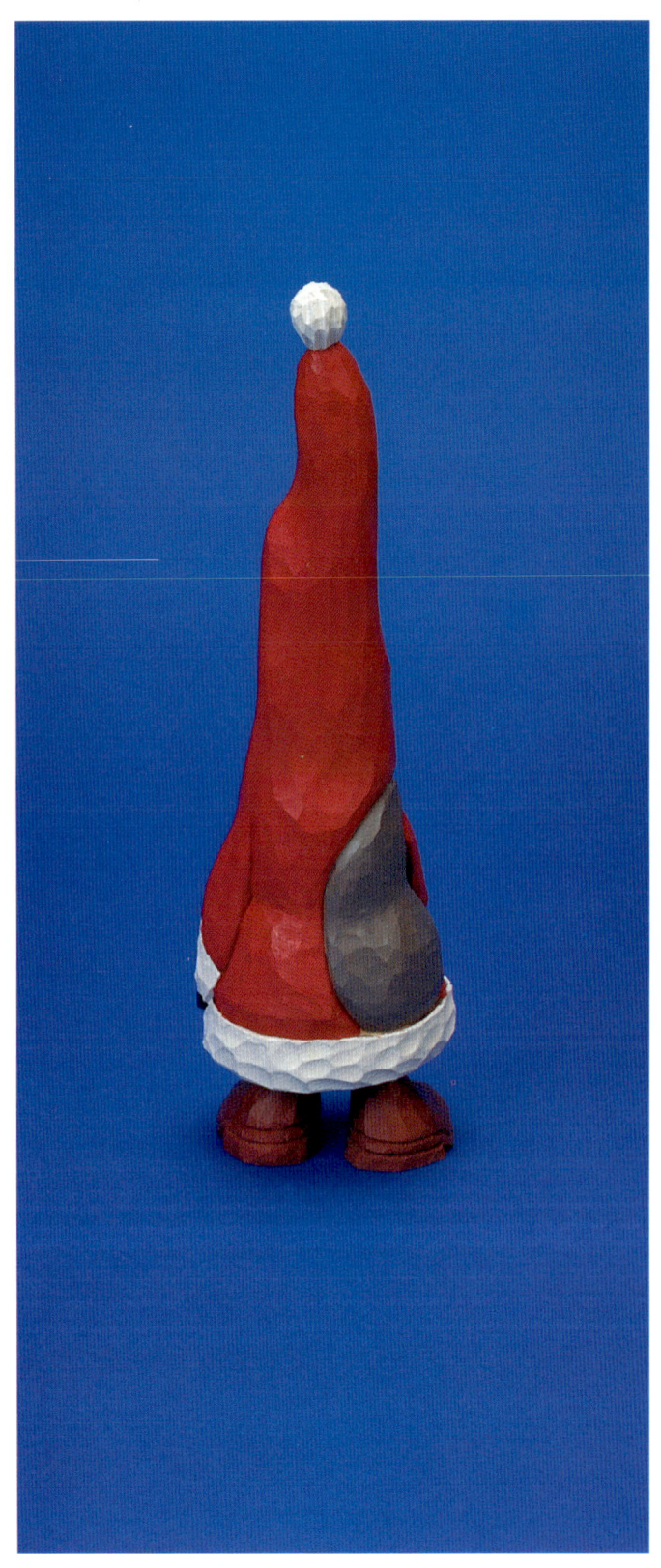

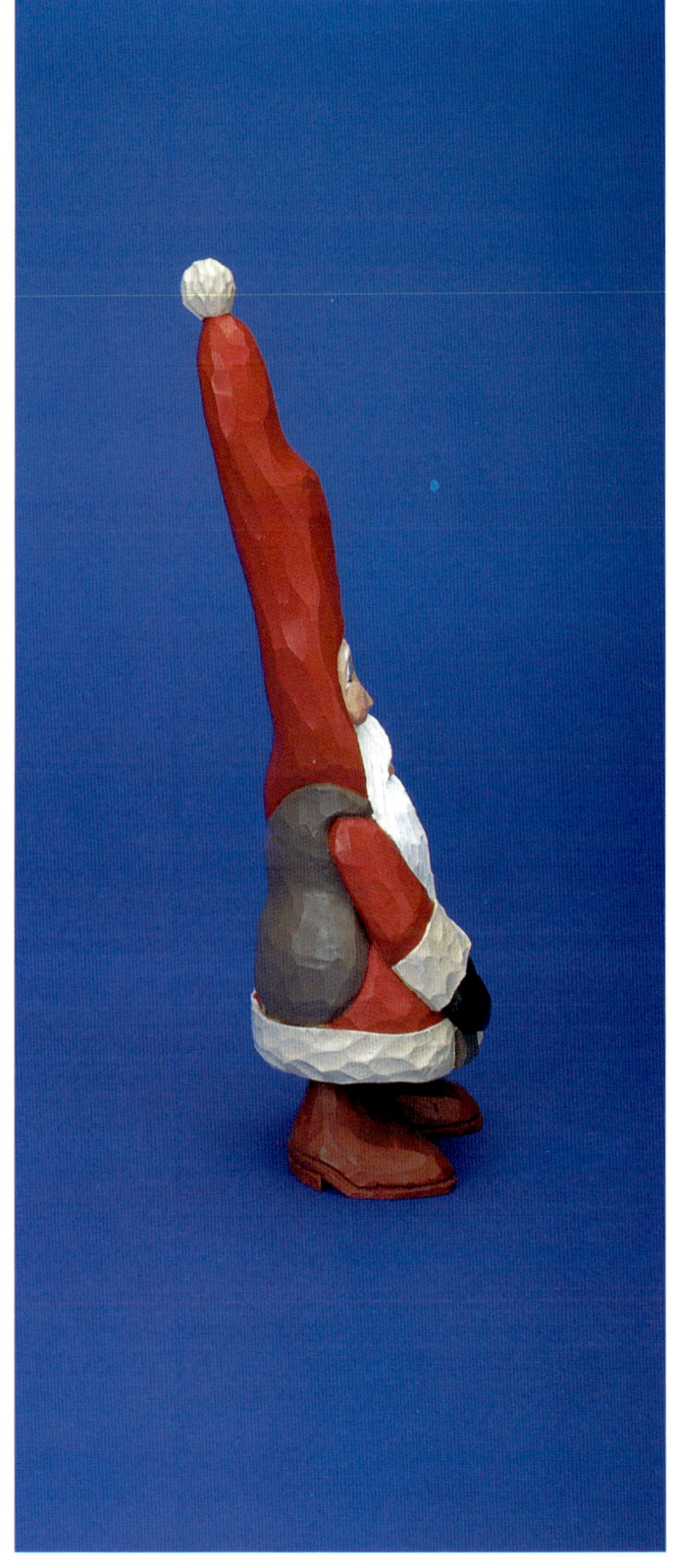

15 Elf and Gnome Patterns. Al Streetman. Once you finish carving your first gnome, the little guy will surely want you to carve some more elfin friends for him! It's a good thing Al Streetman has included 15 different patterns for well-dressed elves and gnomes of all shapes and sizes—drawn up with the beginner in mind, but with plenty of potential for the experienced carver's creativity to build on. With step-by-step instructions and color photography, Al demonstrates how to carve and paint the first project from start to finish. He also provides some helpful general advice about technique, finer details, and painting; his reference charts are handy for any carving. A full-color gallery of finished projects will bring a smile to your face and a spark to your imagination. His laid-back style and straightforward techniques make Al Streetman a pleasure to carve with—enjoy!
Size: 8 1/2" x 11"   112 photos, 15 patterns, reference charts   64pp.
ISBN: 0-7643-0842-4   soft cover $14.95

41 Santa Patterns for Woodcarvers. Al Streetman. 41 exciting, creative new Santa patterns in one book! 41 Santa Patterns for Woodcarvers provides beginning wood carvers with projects which they can accomplish with a minimum of tools and frustration. For the intermediate and advanced carvers it offers a wide assortment of Santas in different poses. One project is followed in a step-by-step, fully illustrated manner, so even the beginner can pick up on basic carving techniques. The patterns in this book are full-size, and include approximate dimensions of the side and front views. Santa carvings are an ever-popular item with carvers, as well as with collectors and people who want them for a touch of warmth in their homes. This book comes at just the right time for those Christmas projects, and will be a delightful resource throughout the year.
Size: 8 1/2" x 11"   50+ color photos, 41 patterns   48pp.
ISBN: 0-88740-632-7   soft cover $12.95

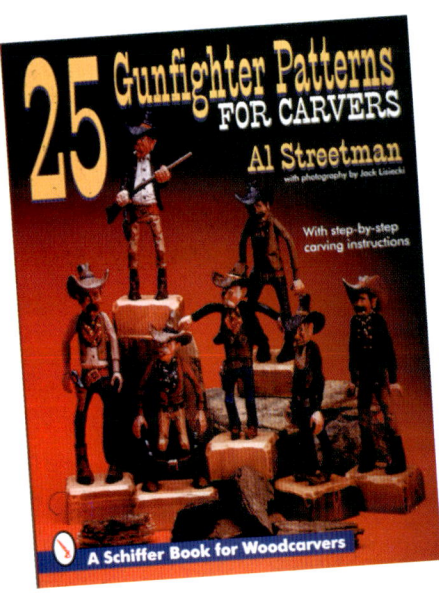

25 Gunfighter Patterns for Carvers. Al Streetman. Al Streetman goes west with a new carving and pattern book. This time he shares the secrets of carving the western gunfighter, and provides the carver with 25 creative patterns...enough for the O.K. Corral and more! Concise instruc-tions take the carver step-by-step through the project, from laying out the pattern to painting the finished work. The book is designed to be used by carvers of all levels, from novice to advanced. The results are delightful figures of which the artist will be proud. This book follows two other well-received carving books by Al Streetman, 41 Santa Patterns for Carvers and 25 Uncle Sam Patterns for Carvers.
Size: 8 1/2" x 11"   150 color photos, 25 patterns   64pp.
ISBN: 0-88740-783-8   soft cover $12.95